OVER THE HILL AND UNDER OBAMACARE:

THE POST-OBAMACARE RETIREMENT PLAN

Over the Hill and Under Obamacare:

The Post-Obamacare Retirement Plan

by Thom L. Cooper & Mitchell J. Adel
Certified* Elder Law Attorneys

* Certified by the National Elder Law Foundation (NELF). NELF is approved by the Ohio Commission on Certification of Attorneys as specialists and by the American Bar Association

ISBN: 978-1-59571-957-7

Designed and published by
Word Association Publishers
205 Fifth Avenue
Tarentum, Pennsylvania 15084

www.wordassociation.com

1.800.827.7903

TABLE OF CONTENTS

PREFACE

"If you put the federal government in charge of the Sahara Desert, in five years there would be a shortage of sand."
—Milton Friedman, Economist

Before a tsunami strikes the shore, the sea recedes and exposes huge areas of the sea floor, creating a deadly spectacle for those who fail to recognize the warning signs of impending danger. Some, aware of the danger before them, alert others and scramble to the highest possible ground in a desperate bid for survival. Others, unaware of what is about to occur, walk out onto the exposed seafloor unknowingly and are swept out to sea with the oncoming tsunami.

If baby boomers fail to adjust their legal, financial, and healthcare planning, the fact that they missed the warning signs won't matter—the government tsunami that strikes will be, in many cases, impossible to overcome. We wrote this book because we believe the warning signs are clearly there, if only you choose to see them. The tsunami is already building in:

- the sea of governmental program failures that threaten our pensions,

- the tax laws that are flooding over traditional estate planning, and

- the waves of healthcare change that will surely affect every American—particularly aging baby boomers and their families—in some way.

We believe that you should not have to lose everything you've spent a lifetime to earn. We believe that you can stay ahead of the waves if you understand and heed the warning signs.

We wrote this book to alert you to the impending dangers. We believe that if you follow us, we can lead you to higher, safer ground where you and your family can protect and preserve your wealth and well-being.

ABOUT THE AUTHORS

Certified* Elder Law **Attorney Thom Cooper** counsels seniors and their families on ways to maximize their independence and minimize the stress and burden placed on their loved ones when a healthcare crisis threatens. Thom believes that everyone, no matter what level of wealth, has something they want to protect, and today it's becoming even more  difficult. Thom has presented educational seminars throughout Ohio for the past 30 years, spreading the message to seniors about ways they can protect and preserve the things they care about most, as he would say, "getting their ducks in a row." Recognized by the highest AVVO rating, 10.0 Superb, Thom was a charter member of the first group of attorneys certified by NELF,* the certification arm of the National Academy of Elder Law Attorneys (NAELA) and has served as the president of the American Association of Trust, Estate and Elder Law Attorneys.

 Certified* Elder Law **Attorney Mitch Adel** has been practicing elder law for over eight years as the managing partner of the statewide elder law firm of Cooper, Adel & Associates. Mitch believes that seniors can protect their retirement and ensure that their surviving spouse is provided for when they are gone.

---

* Certified by the National Elder Law Foundation (NELF). NELF is approved by the Ohio Commission on Certification of Attorneys as specialists and by the American Bar Association.

Mitch's door is always open to support his senior clients and their families in finding benefits and developing strategies to help defray the extraordinary costs of home healthcare, assisted living, and nursing homes. Attorney Adel has provided educational seminars to seniors and their families throughout Ohio. He has also been a guest on 610 WTVN Local News and has written articles for *USA Today*, the *Cincinnati Enquirer*, and Columbus Business First. Attorney Adel is a frequent contributor to *Our Generations Magazine*, Senior Outlook Today, and DepositAccounts.com.

Special Acknowledgements

We believe that this book can make a difference in the lives of many seniors and their families. It has been a work of passion and intense urgency as we struggle to gather and understand the nature of a world that is constantly changing under the weight of government failures, political tax policies, and idealistic, unproven healthcare reforms. We have been fortunate to draw inspiration from a stellar team of individuals who have given their very best to provide our clients, and others who may find our words, with information that goes to the source and not with misinformation that comes from pundits and wonks with an agenda and a blog.

First and foremost, we would like to recognize Lauren C. Cooper, editor and contributing author, who spent untold hours researching, verifying, editing, and writing our book on an unreasonably short timeline. It is impossible to express our gratitude. We also acknowledge Bob Kueppers for his excellent cover photography and design, as well as Mary Roberts and Jessica LoPiccolo who were our models for the cover, and Roy Whited who provided valuable technical assistance during the review process. None of this would have been possible without the amazing support and quick turnaround of the staff from our publisher, Word Association Publishers. We wish to offer our most sincere appreciation to Kendra Williamson and April Urso. Also, a special thanks to the office of Congressman Kevin Brady who gave us permission to use the chart their office developed for our back cover. Finally, we recognize the efforts of our team of contributing authors and thank them for allowing us to bring this book to print. Without their countless hours, it would not have been possible:

- Edward A. Brown, Esq.

- Lauren C. Cooper

- R. Catherine Cooper

- Jonathan Christian Enriquez

- Julian J. Guilfoyle

- Nathaniel Simpson, Esq.

- Duydan H. Vu, Esq.

It is with our sincere gratitude and respect that we offer the labors of our team to you for your consideration. We feel certain that you will agree with us that it was worth the effort.

Authors' Foreward

We believe, as do most Americans today, that the government should be involved in providing retirement benefits and in either managing healthcare benefits or actually providing healthcare benefits for its citizens. Few of us realize, however, what radical social concepts these were just a few generations ago. In fact, government-sponsored retirement and healthcare benefits for the elderly is a fairly modern idea. Certainly at the time our Constitution was signed, these ideas would not have been considered a viable cultural concept. Take a moment to think about the state of medicine when our Constitution was signed in 1787. No one was sure what caused disease. Many believed that illness was a punishment from God or was caused by a miasma, a poisonous cloud containing germs. Operations were crude, at best, and generally infection from a lack of hygiene caused death.[1] Further, the idea of state-sponsored retirement would not have been in the mind of the signers of the Constitution, who represented our largely rural country when the average life expectancy was less than 40 years. For most, the only thing between them and the poorhouse was their family or their wealth.

The idea of state-sponsored retirement was a concept born of the Industrial Revolution and normally credited to Chancellor Bismarck of Germany who, in the 1880s, put forth the radical idea of pensions for workers who reached age 70 as an alternative to the Marxists who were threatening to take control of Europe.[2]

---

1 "Medicine 1750 to 1800," http://www.historylearningsite.co.uk/medicine.html
2 "The History of Retirement, From Early Man to AARP," New York Times, http://www.nytimes.com/1999/03/21/jobs/the-history-of-retirement-from-early-man-to-aarp.html

It should be noted that at that time average life expectancy for males was 43.8 years of age, so little financial risk was involved for Bismarck.[3] It was not until the Industrial Revolution in the U.S. that large numbers of aging workers were "retired" as they were seen as usurping the places of the younger, more productive men who had families to support. The older workers did not want to quit because they had nothing to fall back on to support themselves. The Great Depression made the situation so much worse that President Franklin Roosevelt proposed Social Security in 1935, allowing workers to pay for their own old-age insurance.[4]

The idea of state-sponsored healthcare is even more recent. President Harry Truman is normally the politician first credited with the idea of national healthcare. His later-defeated proposal recognized the responsibility of the federal government to provide "adequate medical care" and the "right to adequate protection from the economic fears of sickness."[5] President Truman's idea was later proposed and expanded by the Medicare program that was enacted by President Lyndon Johnson in the 1960s. In fact, the first Medicare card was issued to Harry Truman. At the time, President Lyndon Johnson said it was "a god-damned crime" that "old folks" could be "barred from a doctor's office or a hospital because they don't have any money."[6] The fact that such a statement would be necessary, particularly by a president, would boggle our minds today.

Obamacare ushers in the next level of evolutionary change and cultural shift, moving the responsibility of medical care for all

3 "Changes in Life Expectancy," http://ajcn.nutrition.org/content/55/6/1196S.full.pdf
4 "The History of Retirement, From Early Man to AARP," http://www.nytimes.com/1999/03/21/jobs/the-history-of-retirement-from-early-man-to-aarp.html
5 "This Day in Truman History," November 19, 1945, President Truman's Proposed Health Program, http://www.trumanlibrary.org/anniversaries/healthprogram.htm
6 "Making Harry Truman's Dream Come True," http://www.lbjlibrary.org/press/making-harry-trumans-dream-come-true

Americans from a largely individual, market-based approach to one of universal entitlement paid by taxes.[7] Obamacare attempts to include all Americans, regardless of age and past illnesses or socioeconomic status, using tax dollars to provide medical care to every one of its citizens. Ultimately, no matter how desirable this evolutionary concept is, as with all those preceding it, the reality must be constantly tested in the harsh social crucible of the country's ability to make it work effectively and to support it.

Many readers may feel that this book is an attack on President Obama, Obamacare,[8] and other politicians involved in passing this healthcare law. That is not our intent. Certainly the President and members of Congress on both sides have a hard enough job trying to respond to the needs of our citizens, and we believe that most politicians are working hard and doing their best in this nearly impossible job. Thus, we leave the politics to others.

It is not our intention as authors to serve as judge and jury over the social morality or the appropriateness of such laws. Rather, we believe our mission is to identify those situations that present a threat to the well-being and access to care of our clients as they age. We believe that there are defensive moves that you can take to legally minimize your personal, financial, and medical losses that may be the unintended consequences of these new laws and regulations as they are implemented in all of their bureaucratic

---

7 "The Affordable Care Act's requirement that certain individuals pay a financial penalty for not obtaining health insurance may reasonably be characterized as a tax. Because the Constitution permits such a tax, it is not our role to forbid it, or to pass upon its wisdom or fairness." Natl. Fedn. of Indep. Business v. Sebelius, 132 S.Ct. 2566, 2600, 183 L.Ed.2d 450 (2012).

8 We have chosen to most often use "Obamacare" to refer to the Patient Protection Affordable Care Act rather than PPACA, ACA, or other government acronyms, as most people recognize that this name represents the class of related laws and regulations under that name. It is not to cast aspersions or make value judgments about it. As a matter of fact, President Obama himself acknowledged that he has no problems if people call it 'ObamaCares.' http://abcnews.go.com/Politics/video/president-obama-call-obamacare-14309723

glory. It is our experience that many of the taxes, laws, and regulations that have preceded this sweeping healthcare reform, have historically had a negative impact on our clients.

We fear that the future may hold an unfortunate reality: "In the decades to come, we will witness millions of elderly Americans, the baby boomers and others, slipping into poverty. Too frail to work, too poor to retire will become the 'new normal' for many elderly Americans."[9] We believe, as elder law attorneys, it is our job to be zealous advocates of our senior clients and their legacy to their heirs, to minimize their liability and to maximize their health and wealth.

---

[9] "The Greatest Retirement Crisis in American History," *Forbes,* http://www.forbes.com/sites/edwardsiedle/2013/03/20/the-greatest-retirement-crisis-in-american-history/

Chapter 1:
The Changing World— An Overview

If baseball umpires had a mission statement, it would read, "you are imperfect, so it is better to be consistently bad than inconsistently good." The thinking is, even if you are calling strikes at ankles, players can adjust if you are consistent. The same could be said about government, especially in America where its citizenry has shown an amazing ability to adapt to a quickly changing world. In the case of the baby boomer, the government has not only made retirement planning difficult and complicated, but also changed the rules in the middle of the game. If boomers fail to adjust their legal, financial, and healthcare planning, the fact that they missed the warning signs won't matter—the incoming government tsunami described in the Preface will be impossible to overcome.

Just as many baby boomers are finally becoming whole after the 2008 financial crisis, three big-government waves are poised to devastate their retirement planning. The first wave has already struck in some areas, and that is the catastrophic failure of government pension management. The second wave has swept away years of planning in the form of new tax laws that change the fundamentals of estate planning. The final wave has yet to reach the shore, but its impact is all but a certainty. That third wave is Obamacare, and its effect on seniors will alter their lives forever.

PART I:
RETIREMENT FOR THE WWII GENERATION VS. BABY BOOMERS

The boomers who base their retirement on what their parents did will experience disastrous results. This is because the WWII generation retired with a basic safety net that covered the most important pillars of retirement: income and healthcare. For the WWII generation, Social Security and Medicare were relatively healthy programs supported by their children. However, as these government promises have grown to an unsustainable level, the young have become less willing to support these programs for the baby boomers. One of the most important aspects of Obamacare is the dramatic shift of this country's attitude toward its elders. Instead of the young supporting their parents, seniors are now being asked to support the youth. In addition, tax laws have been changed, making it more difficult for seniors to protect their wealth, just when they will need it most.

For the 10 thousand baby boomers turning 65 every day until the year 2029,[10] the importance of sound legal, financial, and healthcare planning has reached a new level: it is essential for survival. This is because the pillars of retirement that supported the WWII generation when they retired are quickly eroding, and the warning signs abound. First, the birth of the "pensionless generation" has created a critical need for income and longevity planning. If Social Security or pension benefits are reduced in the future, retirees will be forced to either reign in expenditures or find ways to supplement their incomes. This will also create a greater need to maximize the different income streams that are available to retirees.

---

10 "Baby Boomers Retire," Pew Research Center, http://www.pewresearch.org/daily-number/baby-boomers-retire/

For private-sector employees who have seen their defined *benefit* pension plans (i.e. where an employer promised to pay a specified monthly pension at retirement) converted to defined plans (i.e. 401(k)), their reliance on Social Security will increase just as Social Security becomes less able to provide an income safety net. The U.S. Bureau of Labor Statistics found in 2011 that a mere 10% of private employers offered a defined benefit pension plan to their current employees.[11] Many large employers like Ford and General Motors have actually gone back to their retirees and offered lump sum settlements in lieu of the promised defined benefit retirement pensions.[12] The main reason for the move away from traditional defined pension plans is that the private sector has realized that to stay competitive and survive the wave of the boomers retiring, retirement benefits must be capped. The WWII generation could rely upon their employees for income during retirement. Current retirees are on their own, and one bad decision or a financial crisis can invalidate a lifetime of work.

For public-sector employees, the promises afforded upon retirement are increasingly being renegotiated and reduced. The Pew Charitable Trust Center on the States found that in 2010, only 16 out of 50 state pension systems were funded at the 80% threshold they will need to provide the benefits they promised to public-sector retirees.[13] Overall, the gap between the benefits promised and the pension funds reached a level of $1.38 trillion in fiscal year 2010.[14] Combating this epidemic has proven costly, as Wisconsin Governor Scott Walker can attest after he was recalled because he attempted to end bargaining rights for state employees

---

11 "The Last Private Industry Pension Plans," Bureau of Labor Statistics, http://www.bls.gov/opub/ted/2013/ted_20130103.htm

12 "GM Outsources Pensions, Offers Lump-Sum Buyouts," USA Today, http://content.usatoday.com/communities/driveon/post/2012/06/gm-pension-buyouts/1#.Ugh0rxbC_VM

13 "The Widening Gap," The Pew Charitable Trusts, http://www.pewstates.org/research/data-visualizations/the-widening-gap-85899377237

14 http://www.pewstates.org/research/reports/the-widening-gap-update-85899398241

so he could rein in the state's burgeoning retirement-funding gap. In Ohio, Governor John Kasich attempted to reduce government retiree benefits through a bill known as Senate Bill 5, just to watch voters roundly defeat it in the ballot box. While unpopular, it is reasonable for public-sector retirees to expect that, as these pension deficits continue to balloon, their benefits will be on the chopping block.

As private companies and public pensions continue to renegotiate current and future income benefits, the federal government has decided to fundamentally alter the healthcare promise it made to seniors almost fifty years ago. Obamacare is the most sweeping healthcare law to ever impact the United States. This is because, while Medicare has provided a healthcare safety net for seniors and Medicaid has provided healthcare protection for the impoverished, Obamacare affects every individual in America.

Seniors will feel the brunt of Obamacare because they pay the great majority of it. For Medicare recipients, reimbursement rates to healthcare providers will be reduced to the tune of $716 billion over the next 10 years.[15] This is accomplished by provisions in Obamacare that scale back the reimbursement rate paid to doctors and hospitals for care provided to Medicare recipients. Today, Medicare reimburses, on average, about 81% of what private insurance pays.[16] The Medicaid reimbursement rate averages about 56%.[17] Obamacare reduces the Medicare reimbursement rate, making it more in-line with the Medicaid reimbursement rate. This results in the largest share of the cost to pay for Obamacare coming at the expense of seniors at about $455 billion over 10 years.[18]

15 Nick J. Tate, The Obamacare Survivial Guide, 18.
16 Richard Liuag, Obamacare Bootcamp, Lesson 2, min. 1:55.
17 Ibid., min. 2:00.
18 Tate, Obamacare Survival Guide, 141.

Seniors who currently enjoy Medicare Advantage programs, which allow Medicare enrollees to supplement their basic Medicare coverage with private insurance, will have their benefits reduced by about $136 billion over 10 years.[19] In addition, Obamacare provides financial incentives to healthcare providers who under-utilize care and penalizes the healthcare providers it deems are over-utilizing care.[20] Finally, Obamacare creates a fifteen-member unelected board called the Independent Payment Advisory Board (IPAB), whose main job it is to oversee further cuts in what Medicare pays to healthcare providers.[21] Should this board enact cuts unfavorable to the American people, a small miracle must occur to overturn the cuts. That is because the only way the cuts are repealed is if one of three criteria are met: the cuts are overruled by a three-fifths super majority in Congress, Congress creates an alternative similar in net-cost reduction, or Congress files for an appeal between January 1 and February 1 of 2017.[22] The net result of Obamacare's impact on seniors will be increased cost and reduced accessibility to healthcare providers when there are more seniors than ever who will require care.

PART II:
THE THREE BIG WAVES POSED TO HIT BABY BOOMERS' RETIREMENT

The First Wave: Failed Government Programs and Pension Systems

For the WWII generation, the first pillar of retirement was the reliability of their pensions. However, as government mismanagement has eroded the foundations over time, this pillar

---

19 Ibid.
20 Liuag, Obamacare Bootcamp, Lesson 2, min. 4:25.
21 Ibid., min. 5:41.
22 Ibid., min. 6:26.

is posed to crumble under the weight of baby boomers. The greatest attribute that pensions provide, whether public or private, is that you cannot outlive them. They provide the retiree a guaranteed income stream for life. This is also the pension's most difficult hurdle to overcome. For generations, public pensions, whether at the city, state, or federal level have provided the majority of income security for government retirees. Private-sector retirees have relied on private pensions and/or Social Security to provide the income safety net. Guaranteed income for life places an unbelievable burden on the pension's contributors because they are not only contributing to their own retirements, but also funding current retirees' benefits. When boomers are collecting Social Security, for example, most of the benefits they receive will not be their individual contributions, but the contributions of current workers. This is why the Social Security Trustees estimated in their 2013 Annual Report that the trust fund will be exhausted by 2033. [23]Social Security is simply paying out higher benefits than they are collecting or have saved. Now, what happens in 2033 if the federal government fails to "fix" the program before then? Social Security will be able to pay only an estimated 77% of the benefits promised.[24] That figure is based on what contributors are projected to pay into Social Security at the time. The end result of this is that Social Security will no longer be able to supplement benefits because the Social Security Trust Fund, which has collected excess payments for years, will be exhausted. In addition, the Social Security Administration found that "a man reaching age 65 today can expect to live, on average, until age 84. A woman turning age 65 today can expect to live, on average, until age 86. About one out of every four 65-year-olds today will live past age 90, and one out of 10 will live past age 95."[25] The perfect storm is gathering to

---

23 "A Summary of the 2013 Annual Reports," Social Security and Medicare Boards of Trustees, http://www.ssa.gov/oact/trsum/
24 Ibid.
25 "Calculators: Life Expectancy," Social Security Administration, http://www.ssa.gov/planners/lifeexpectancy.htm

impact Social Security recipients during their lifetime; they will retire, live longer, and will have to do so with less income.

Longevity is not the only factor putting strain on pension systems. The investment return assumption built into these programs is another formidable culprit behind pension underfunding. This is because the investment return assumption dictates how much public employees and taxpayers must contribute to these pension systems to keep them solvent, and it is terribly difficult to adjust. If this estimate is too high, current contributors are underfunding their pension system leaving a greater burden on future recipients and taxpayers. The National Association of State Retirement Administrators conducted a study of 126 public pensions in August of 2012 and found that "while 8.0% remains the predominant rate assumption, the average is 7.8%."[26] The contributors to these pension systems were contributing based on the calculation that they would yield an annual return of 7.8% on their investment. If the pension fund yields less than this investment return assumption, the gap between the pension fund level and the benefits promised increases. One way to alleviate some of this strain in a low-yield environment is to decrease the assumption. The problem faced by politicians is that if you reduce this assumption to a more applicable rate, you have to either raise contributions from working members and/or taxpayers, or reduce the benefits paid to current and/or future retirees. Because a politician's most important job is to get reelected, the highly controversial steps required to right these pension systems has become an impossible position to represent. Therefore, in most cases these investment return assumptions are left unchanged. An underfunded pension system combined with more retirees who are living longer has created an enormous amount of uncertainty for public-sector retirees.

---

26 http://www.nasra.org/files/Issue%20Briefs/NASRAInvReturnAssumptBrief.pdf?p=4

If they are to protect themselves, public-sector retirees must take note of the increasing amount of pension funds that are failing across our nation. One of the first cases that prompted national coverage occurred in Pritchard, Alabama. Like many cities and states across our nation, for more than a decade Pritchard had been grappling with the problem of paying out more benefits while bringing in fewer contributions and earning less of a return on investment. The city's decline began in the 1970s as unemployment rose and the tax base dwindled.[27] Faced with the scenario of reducing benefits or reducing services provided in the community, Pritchard decided to do neither. After seeking bankruptcy protection twice, the pension fund was finally depleted in 2009.[28] Backed into a corner with few options at its disposal, the city decided to break an Alabama state law that required it to pay its retirees full benefits, and discontinued sending their retirees pension checks altogether.[29] In an effort to secure at least some of their promised retirement benefits, a majority of Pritchard retirees accepted a two-thirds reduction of their pension payments.

More recently, a city much larger, but plagued by the same systemic problems, has made the headlines for similar reasons. In July 2013, Detroit, once a symbol of America's industrial prowess, declared the largest municipal bankruptcy in American history. Detroit's story is especially worrisome due to the commonality it shares with many cities across the nation. Industrial cities like Detroit have had tremendous difficulty adapting to a new world. Wary of cutting benefits to retirees and municipal services, Detroit attempted to curtail revenue gaps by raising taxes, but that just made it more susceptible to competition from other cities, states, and countries. While Detroit's liabilities continued to accumulate, government officials were planning as if the city would either

27 "Alabama Town's Failed Pension is a Warning," New York Times, http://www.nytimes.com/2010/12/23/business/23prichard.html?pagewanted=all&_r=0
28 Ibid.
29 Ibid.

retain or even grow in population. However, from its peak in 1950, the population of Detroit fell by more than half, from more than 1.5 million residents in 1950 to a little more than 700,000 in 2012.[30] Despite this reality, the city's expenditure cuts continually lagged behind the losses they experienced in revenue. Faced with more than $20 billion of debt, the city declared bankruptcy.

Now, this does not mean that Detroit, having filed for bankruptcy protection, will be able to wipe away this debt. Emergency manager Kevyn Orr has proposed paying bondholders just 10 cents on the dollar for unsecured bonds and imposed similar cuts to healthcare and pension benefits for retirees.[31] What Detroit wants to do is reduce the payments on this debt to a level it believes it can actually pay. Certainly, this did not come as good news to bondholders, but with the alternative being that they receive nothing, they may find it acceptable. However, for retirees who are counting on these pension and healthcare benefits, a reduction, especially one as substantial as being discussed, is a nonstarter. Simply put, most of them will find it difficult to survive. This is because their pension is their retirement; they do not have a fallback.

The real problem that these pensions face is that they are unfunded. Like Social Security, but to a worse degree, the basic thought is that they will always have a contributing base for the retirees. However, like Social Security, most city and state pension systems do not have an adequate trust fund set aside to compensate for changes like population shifts, high unemployment, or, in Detroit's case, a failure to even collect taxes that the city is owed.[32] The plight of a

30 Raw Data: Detroit's Population Lowest since 1914," Detroit Free Press, http://www.freep. com/article/20130728/OPINION05/307280034/detroit-population-decline-loss
31 "11 Charts that Show Why Detroit is Falling Apart and Headed for Bankruptcy," Business Insider, http://www.businessinsider.com/11-charts-that-show-why-detroit-is-falling-apart-and-heading-for-bankruptcy-2013-6?op=1
32 "Proposal for Creditors," City of Detroit, http://www.clickondetroit.com/blob/view/-/20572572/data/1/-/li92ur/-/City-of-Detroit-Proposal-for-Creditors.pdf

public-sector retiree could not be worse: they have contributed for their working lives into a fund that, when they retire, is exhausted.

THE SECOND WAVE: NEW TAX LAWS THAT WILL CHANGE THE FUNDAMENTALS OF ESTATE PLANNING

The second wave poised to impact seniors is the changing tax environment surrounding their estate plans. The importance of planning, and the subsequent maintenance of that plan, has never been more important for seniors than it is today. While some concerns remain the same, like having assets transfer seamlessly at death, seniors must now also plan around failing government-managed pension systems, a changing tax atmosphere, and massive changes to their healthcare coverage.

One of the most prevalent mistakes made by seniors today is the failure to create a comprehensive estate plan that incorporates all of the individual planning tools they have accumulated over time. Most of us accrue these planning tools along the way as certain challenges present themselves. When we are younger, we often purchased term life insurance in order to provide for dependent children or pay an outstanding mortgage. When we reach retirement, some of us take a reduced pension to help provide income for our spouse should we predecease them. Some of us create legal documents like powers of attorney to allow our trusted loved ones to walk in our shoes if we become unable to act. However, few of us take all these tools and incorporate them into an overall strategy. When laws change, those with a piecemeal approach to planning are especially vulnerable because generally they are not maintaining and reviewing their various tools as often as they should. Put plainly, what may have worked ten years ago may not be the best planning technique available today. Worse, in some cases, the previous planning may actually be detrimental to the individual.

The estate tax, also known as the death tax, is a tax levied on an estate if it surpasses a certain level of exemption. Many view the estate tax as an immoral tax because it is effectively a double tax. With some exceptions, for example the growth in tax-deferred or tax-exempt investments, people have already paid taxes on assets they have at death. When they die, should their estate exceed the exempt amount set by state or federal government, their beneficiaries will owe an estate or death tax. For example, up until January 1, 2013, the state of Ohio taxed estates at death (some exclusions applied, like life insurance) if the assets were above $338,333. If the estate was above the exemption, taxes were due at a rate of 6% up to $500,000.[33] For estates above $500,000, Ohio citizens paid 6% on the amount between $338,333 and $500,000, then 7% on everything above $500,000.[34] In addition to Ohio, three other states have either repealed or are scheduled to repeal their estate or inheritance taxes.[35]

While the federal estate tax exemption was notably higher, so were its tax rates. For example, in 2007 the federal exemption was $2 million with a taxable rate of 18% for estates that exceeded the exemption; if the estate exceeded $3 million, that tax rate jumped to 45%.[36] Although it was certainly not their only concern, the estate tax served as a primary motivation for many seniors to create an estate plan.

---

33 "Tax Change—Ohio Estate Tax is Ending" Ohio Department of Taxation, http://www.tax.ohio.gov/estate.aspx
34 Ibid.
35 "Survey of Estate, Inheritance, and Gift Taxes," Research Department Minnesota House of Representatives, http://www.house.leg.state.mn.us/hrd/pubs/estatesurv.pdf
36 Darian B. Jacobson, et al., "The Estate Tax Ninety Years and Counting," http://www.irs.gov/pub/irs-soi/ninetyestate.pdf

When Congress and President Obama struck a deal to end the "fiscal cliff" fiasco, one of the major changes that impacted retirees related to the federal estate tax. The federal estate tax exemption, which was raised to over $5 million in 2012 but was scheduled to sunset to $1 million in 2013, was again increased to $5.25 million in the deal. Also in 2013, the concept of portability was introduced. Portability allows the second spouse to use any of the exemption of the first spouse that was not used at first death. With the stroke of a pen, many estate plans were rendered partially or totally irrelevant or fatally flawed because they were now avoiding a tax that was no longer applicable. Whereas previously even modest households could owe a state and/or federal estate tax, now the estate of a married couple would owe the federal government only if they had accrued more than $10.5 million in assets. Further, because of portability, now seniors don't have to use advanced techniques to preserve exemptions for both spouses; they are entitled to it automatically so long as an estate tax filing is made for the estate.

The problem becomes clearer when one looks at what was being sacrificed to achieve the planner's goals. Capital gains is the tax levied on the difference between what you originally paid for an asset and what you sold it for later. Because the capital gains tax rate has historically been lower than the estate tax rate, oftentimes seniors and their planners sacrificed paying capital gains tax to avoid state or federal estate taxes. With portability and a higher exemption in effect, fewer of us need to worry about estate tax. However, capital gains tax rates are going to increase for some due to a new 3.8% Medicare surtax.[37] For many of us, it will be advantageous to direct our planning efforts toward capital gains tax savings. As the third wave approaches, baby boomers are going to find that they need to save every dollar they have if they mean to survive Obamacare.

---

37 "A Texpayer's Guide to 2013," *Fidelity Invesments,* https://www.fidelity.com/viewpoints/personal-finance/taxpayers-guide

OUR VIEW: Obamacare is only part of the picture that will affect your ability to take care of yourself as you age. New tax laws that have gone largely unnoticed with all of the focus on Obamacare have the potential to derail your planning by reducing the funds you have available to live comfortably and to afford the healthcare that we believe that you will need to pay for privately. Therefore, it is imperative that you keep your eye on the prize with respect to the recent tax law changes. For the better part of 30 years, the general rule of thumb was to get assets *out* of an estate in order to avoid state and federal estate taxes. Many seniors did so at the cost of paying additional capital gains tax simply because it was the lesser of two evils. However, as the capital gains tax rate has increased and the federal government raised the estate tax exemption to a level that affects far fewer families, it is our view that most of those prior estate plans are now outdated, and the focus should shift from estate tax avoidance to minimizing capital gains tax. Where it was once advantageous for seniors to get assets *out* of their estates to avoid estate tax, now the opposite holds true: seniors most likely will want to keep assets *in* their estates to save capital gains tax. These new tax changes have created a need for almost everyone who had previously done estate planning to review their plan and modify it accordingly. This will be discussed more extensively in Chapter 3.

The Third Wave:
Massive Changes to the U.S. Healthcare System

Obamacare is the third wave poised to strike baby boomers. But it is more than that, as Obamacare will impact every American in one form or another. The healthcare law affects the young and the old, the rich and the poor, the insured and the uninsured. The stated goal or mission statement for the Affordable Care Act (ACA), or as it is popularly known, Obamacare, is to provide quality, affordable healthcare for all Americans.[38] Like many government programs, the devil is in the details. With nearly 500 provisions in the ACA,[39] it is imperative for seniors to know how to navigate Obamacare so that they can both access and pay for care, because they bear the brunt of the cost and of the "savings."

Following the Supreme Court's decision allowing for major provisions within the ACA to become law, the Congressional Budget Office (CBO) and Joint Committee on Taxation (JCT) revised the cost of Obamacare to $1.363 trillion for the period of 2014–2023.[40] Still, in the same report released by the CBO and JCT, they determined that the Affordable Care Act "reduced deficits over the next 10 years and in the subsequent decade."[41]

This led to the big question: How can the federal government provide healthcare coverage to 30 million uninsured; mandate additional, previously uncovered benefits for many; and simultaneously reduce the debt?

---

38 http://www.gpo.gov/fdsys/pkg/BILLS-111hr3590enr/pdf/BILLS-111hr3590enr.pdf, 12.
39 Tate, Obamacare Survival Guide, xviii.
40 "CBO's Estimate of the Net Budgetary Impact of the Affordable Care Act's Health Insurance Coverage Provisions Has Not Changed Much Over Time," Congressional Budget Office, http://www.cbo.gov/publication/44176
41 Ibid.

Well, the fact that is they may not. Let's look to history for guidance. In the 1960s the House and Ways Committee estimated that Medicare would cost the American taxpayer $12 billion by 1990. In 1990 the actual cost of Medicare was $98 billion.[42] Because it directly applies to practically every American not on Medicare, the scope of Obamacare greatly exceeds that of Medicare, making cost assumptions even more difficult to project. In addition, every time there is an ACA waiver granted, whether it is given to Congress, the states of Nevada or New Hampshire, or a company like McDonald's, the projected revenue to support the program is reduced accordingly. However, while costs may overrun, there is no denying that the ACA will generate a substantial amount of revenue through revenue cuts to seniors' Medicare programs and cuts to Medicare providers. The main source of this funding is Medicare, with Medicare repayment rates and the Medicare Advantage Plan absorbing the highest level of cuts. Further, the full scales of these "savings" are not yet known because of the IPAB and the frightening level of power granted to them.

The Independent Payment Advisory Group, or IPAB, which is charged with finding ways to reduce Medicare costs, has been the subject of some of the most intense criticism surrounding Obamacare. Howard Dean, a physician, former Democratic presidential candidate, and healthcare reform advocate called it "essentially a healthcare rationing body" and called for its repeal.[43] He stated, "by setting doctor reimbursement rates for Medicare and determining which procedures and drugs will be covered and at what price, the IPAB will be able to stop certain treatments its members do not favor by simply setting rates to levels where no doctor or hospital will perform them."[44] Many

42 "U.S. Health Plans Have History of Cost Overruns," Washington Times, http://www.washingtontimes.com/news/2009/nov/18/health-programs-have-history-of-cost-overruns/?page=all
43 The Affordable Care Act's Rate-Setting Won't Work," Wall Street Journal, http://online.wsj.com/article/SB10001424127887324110404578628542498014414.html
44 Ibid.

common procedures, from knee replacements to mammograms to dialysis will be put under the scrutiny of the IPAB. The concern is that they will end procedures that they deem elective in order to end the "overutilization" of our healthcare system, as the authors of the ACA put it. Part of the reason our healthcare system is so expensive, however, is due to the level of care it provides. Innovative procedures are costly, especially at the outset, until they are streamlined and the rates of success improve. Remember, overturning decisions made by this board is not an easy solution. Voters cannot reign in this board because they are not elected officials; rather, they are appointed by the president and confirmed by the Senate. In an age when Congress rarely agrees about anything (in fact, the Congress ending in 2012 was the least productive Congress ever [45]), this governing body must have a three-fifths majority to overturn these recommendations or they automatically go into effect.[46] In part because the IPAB cannot have any practicing physicians on its fifteen-member board, the American Society for Anesthesiologists, for one, opposes the IPAB and has even cofounded the IPAB Repeal Coalition that represents more than 350,000 physicians and patients.[47]

If there is good news regarding the IPAB, it is that the IPAB has now been delayed through 2015, the first year the IPAB's spending recommendations could have gone into effect.[48] The trigger for the IPAB's spending recommendations to take effect with its draconian spending cuts is based on the following idea: If Medicare's per-

45 "Capitol Hill Least Productive Congress Ever: 112th Fought About Everything," Washington Times, http://www.washingtontimes.com/news/2013/jan/9/capitol-hill-least-productive-congress-ever-112th-/?page=all
46 Tate, Obamacare Survival Guide, 145–146.
47 "Congressional Republican leaders Decline to Offer IPAB Appointments," American Society of Anesthesiologists, http://asahq.org/For-Members/Advocacy/Washington-Alerts/Congressional-Republican-Leaders-Decline-to-Offer-IPAB-Appointments.aspx
48 "As Health-care Costs Slow, IPAB's Launch is Delayed," Washington Post, http://www.washingtonpost.com/blogs/wonkblog/wp/2013/05/03/as-health-care-costs-slow-ipabs-launch-is-delayed/

enrollee spending exceeds the growth of inflation as measured by the Consumer Price Index (CPI), how likely is it that inflation will under pace expenses?[49] Let's look to a historical comparison of Medicare's costs versus inflation.

Figure 1-A: Growth in Medicare per Enrollee Spending vs. CPI (1980-2011)[50]

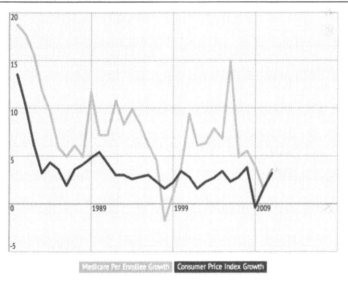

Annual percent change in Medicare per enrolle spending and Consumer Price Index (1980-2011)

Sources: National Health Expenditures Historical Data. Bureau of Labor Statistics

Figure 1-A shows the CPI in red and the Medicare's per-patient growth rate in yellow since the 1980s. Clearly, Medicare's growth in spending is almost always ahead of inflation. Therefore, it is a reasonable assumption that the Medicare recipients will be experiencing the IPAB's recommendations for cuts before long.

---

49 Ibid.
50 Ibid.

Even ahead of the IPAB, there are already cuts in place that will drastically cut Medicare benefits and increase the cost of healthcare to seniors. Medicare Part C, or Medicare Advantage, is designed to allow Medicare recipients to purchase healthcare plans run by private health insurance companies and regulated by the government. Insurers are paid a per-enrollee reimbursement fee from Medicare, so if they are able to provide services for less than this fee, they make a profit. The ACA generates more than 10% (or $136 billion) of its entire revenue between 2010 and 2019 by reducing this subsidy paid to private insurance companies.[51] Because reducing the subsidy narrows the margins for profitability, the entire program could potentially be in jeopardy. This is again reliant upon the federal government enforcing these lower reimbursements.[52] If you are considering or already have Medicare Advantage Plans, you are going to have to closely monitor the program and adjust your healthcare plan quickly and accordingly if the planned cutbacks are implemented.

OUR VIEW: With the drastic reductions contemplated for the Medicare Advantage Plans, we are recommending that our clients consider switching from the Advantage Plans back to traditional Medicare supplement insurance policies.

---

51 Tate, Obamacare Survival Guide, 141.

52 Under heavy pressure, the Centers for Medicare and Medicaid Services reversed itself in April 2013, when it raised Medicare Advantage payment rates 3.3% in 2014 from a scheduled cut of 2.3% that was announced in February 2013. An increasing amount of seniors have been shifting to Medicare Advantage Plans because they provide for caps in out-of-pocket expenses, help pay for co-pays and coinsurance, and can be less expensive than Medigap plans (Medicare Supplements). In fact, the Kaiser Family Foundation, a leader in health policy analysis, found that in 2012 some 27% of Medicare beneficiaries were enrolled in Medicare Advantage Plans. This was more than double its enrollment in 2003, when only 13% of Medicare recipients elected to purchase part C plans. "Medicare Advantage Fact Sheet," The Kaiser Family Foundation, http://kff.org/medicare/fact-sheet/medicare-advantage-fact-sheet/

The end result of the government tsunami poised to strike retirees and baby boomers is that their lives just became infinitely more complex. To survive, they must have the right advisors, to self-educate, and to make sound legal, financial, and healthcare decisions. As contrasted previously, the WWII generation was able to rely upon government pension programs, a relatively stable tax-planning environment, and Medicare to cover their healthcare costs. Baby boomers will not enjoy this stable environment through retirement. They will need to monitor their public pensions and Social Security and find alternative ways to generate income if either are reduced or threatened. They must adjust their current estate plans or work with advisors in the know to create estate plans that reflect and take advantage of these changes to the tax code. Finally, to ensure they can access and pay for care, they will need to know how best to supplement their Medicare benefits and obtain care that may no longer be covered. Otherwise, they might as well walk into the sea and enjoy the spectacle, because they are oblivious of the impending tsunami.

The Takeaway: Lessons Learned

- Review your existing estate plan or develop an estate plan with experienced, trusted advisors so you can maximize the funds you have available, live comfortably, and pay for quality healthcare.

- Monitor changes that might affect you with regard to your pension and Social Security. Seek advice about how you can maintain a stable income throughout the rest of your life.

Chapter 2:

Obamacare And Its Impact On Seniors

This chapter will look at the nuts and bolts of Obamacare, what it will mean for Americans, and, most importantly, what it means for seniors. In doing so, it is important to address a few issues from the start about what Obamacare does not do. These three ideas will be important to keep in mind as you read more about what effects Obamacare will have on you and your family.

Three Things Every Senior Must Remember When Planning for Obamacare

#1: Obamacare was not designed to help seniors.

Obamacare was designed to assist younger Americans, not seniors. This is fundamentally important to understanding the program and how it will affect the care that seniors receive.

#2: Obamacare is not designed to increase the availability of or access to healthcare.

Obamacare was not designed to make it easier to find care, and it is not designed to increase access to care. Obamacare, as it was enacted, is solely a method of increasing adoption of health insurance by Americans. While this may lower costs and increase use of healthcare by Americans, it may in fact come at the expense of access.

#3: Obamacare may be detrimental to the care seniors will receive.

Obamacare may have long-term impacts on both the availability and quality of care that seniors receive under Medicare, so it is important to begin planning now to avoid any of the pitfalls that arise as Obamacare is implemented.

With these three fundamental ideas in mind, we will look at Obamacare from two drastically different perspectives: before retirement and after retirement. Part I looks at the effects of Obamacare on its intended demographic, Americans who have not yet reached Medicare eligibility age. We will look at the individual mandate, at premium assistance and the Medicaid expansion, and finally at limits on coverage imposed under the law. The employer mandate contains far too many complexities and pitfalls to be adequately addressed in this book and will thus be left for a later date. Part II will discuss the impact of Obamacare on seniors who are eligible for Medicare—even though it was not designed for them, it will significantly affect them. The impact will be felt most significantly by seniors in three ways: a decline in Medicare Advantage Plans, increased costs of healthcare, and decreased access to healthcare for seniors.

In the end this chapter we will answer your question of "How will Obamacare affect me?" by introducing you to the two questions that all seniors will be asking themselves post-Obamacare: How will I afford care? How will I access care?

PART I:
OBAMACARE'S IMPACT BEFORE RETIREMENT

Possibly the most overlooked aspect of Obamacare is who it is meant to benefit. It was not designed as a program for seniors. It is a program designed with a narrow objective: to increase the number of working-age Americans with health insurance. Obamacare aims to accomplish this objective by using both punishments and rewards. In essence, it is a three-pronged approach to individual adoption of health insurance:

> *1. Mandate that larger employers provide health insurance for full-time employees.*

> *2. Mandate that all individuals purchase health insurance or face penalties.*

> *3. Offer Medicaid expansion and premium assistance for those individuals who cannot afford private healthcare.*

The law also seeks to increase the adoption of health insurance by creating exchanges that are intended to make it easier for individuals to shop for and purchase the required health coverage. The exchanges, run by the state or federal government, will be marketplaces where consumers can go to find information and sign up for Obamacare-qualified insurance plans. By having this "one-stop shop," the law is intended to simplify the purchase of health insurance.

PENALTIES FOR INDIVIDUALS

The primary method by which Obamacare seeks to increase insurance adoption rates for individuals not covered by an employer-sponsored insurance plan is through the individual mandate. What this means is that individuals who fail to obtain a qualifying health insurance plan will face penalties from the IRS.[53] These penalties are designed to phase in gradually over the course of the next few years, beginning on January 1, 2014, and will be fully implemented in 2016.[54]

Figure 2–A outlines the mechanics of how individuals will be penalized under Obamacare for not maintaining the mandated minimum amount of health insurance. The penalty is based on a designated percentage of the individual's income, but there is a "cap," or a maximum penalty that can be imposed on an individual for not having health insurance.

Figure 2–A: The Obamacare Penalty Rollout [55]

Year	Penalty	Cap
2014	$95 per household member or 1% of income over IRS filing minimum, whichever is greater	$285
2015	$325 per household member or 2% of income over IRS filing minimum, whichever is greater	$975
2016	$695 per household member or 2.5% of income over IRS filing minimum, whichever is greater	$2,085

The first thing to note about these penalties is that they will generally be lower than the cost of health insurance. The mere existence of the penalty will cause many individuals to purchase health insurance. The general nature of Americans is to follow the law, and many will choose to purchase insurances merely to avoid the stigma of being non-compliant. The goal behind Obamacare's penalties is to

53 Tate, Obamacare Survival Guide, 64-65.
54 Ibid.
55 The table was created using information from Ibid.

create an incentive for individuals who do not currently have health insurance to purchase insurance through the exchanges, not to force individuals into purchasing health insurance. Increasing the number of insured persons will result in increased utilization of healthcare by previously uninsured persons.

PREMIUM ASSISTANCE AND EXPANSION OF MEDICAID

In order to make it easier for individuals to comply with Obamacare regulations, the law also provides for the expansion of Medicaid and health insurance premium assistance for eligible individuals. Whether an individual is eligible for assistance and, if so, through which program depends entirely on his or her family's income compared to the Federal Poverty Limit (FPL). The FPL is released annually and is dependent on family size. Figure 2–B illustrates the eligibility limits for either Medicaid or premium assistance based on the income for a family of two and a family of four, according to the 2013 FPL.

Figure 2–B: Obamacare Premium Assistance and Medicaid Expansion Eligibility[56]

Assistance Eligiblity	Income Minimum			Income Maximum		
	% of FLP	$ Based on Family of 2	$ Based on Family of 4	% of FLP	$ Based on Family of 2	$ Based on Family of 4
Medicaid	0%	$0	$0	133%	$20,628	$29,327
Premium Assistance	133%	$20,628	$29,328	400%	$62,040	$88,200
None	400%	$62,041	$88,201	>$400%	N/A	N/A

---

56 Ibid., 62: "2013 Poverty Guidelines," Medicaid, http://www.medicaid-CHIP-Program-Information/By-Topics/Eligibility/Downloads/2013-Federal-Poverty-level-charts.pdf, Aug 23, 2013

As the chart shows, under Obamacare, many Americans will qualify for premium assistance, specifically those making between 133% and 400% of the FPL. These individuals will qualify for premium subsidies on a sliding scale. The subsidies are set by the maximum percentage of income that can be spent on health coverage under the law. For a family at 400% of the FPL, this is 9.5% of income, or $698 per month. This declines to 2% of income at 133% of FPL, or $49. Those individuals making between 133% and 400% will fall somewhere between 2% and 9.5% of income. For those making above 400% of FPL, Obamacare provides for no subsidies of health coverage. These rules are fairly straightforward, but determining the type of assistance and coverage that will be available for those making under 133% is far more complicated.

For individuals between 0 and 133% of the Federal Poverty Line (FPL), Obamacare provides for expanded Medicaid coverage to provide no-cost healthcare for qualified individuals. However, due to the Supreme Court ruling in *National Federation of Independent Businesses v. Sebelius*, expanded Medicaid may not be available to all Americans since the expansion of Medicaid is no longer mandatory for every state under Obamacare.[57] Instead, states choose whether or not they will accept the additional funding and thereafter expand their Medicaid. Many states have yet to expand their Medicaid programs. The map in Figure 2–C illustrates which states are moving forward with Medicaid expansion, which states are still debating it, and which states have chosen to reject the proposal as of October 2013.

---

57 NFIB v. Sebelius, 132 S. Ct. 603 (2011).

Figure 2–C: The Medicaid Expansion[58]

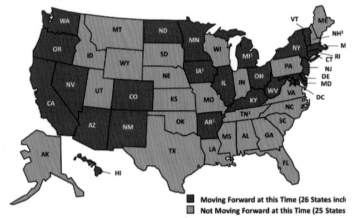

Current Status of State Medicaid Expansion Decisions, October 22, 2013

■ Moving Forward at this Time (26 States incl
▦ Not Moving Forward at this Time (25 States

NOTES: 1 - Exploring an approach to Medicaid expansion likely to require waiver approval. 2- Discussion of a special session being called or Medicaid expansion.
SOURCES: State decisions on the Medicaid expansion as of October 22, 2013. Based on data from the Centers for Medicare and Medicaid

Standards set by some states have left a significant coverage gap for those who fall within certain income ranges. In states that have chosen to retain the old standards for Medicaid, many Americans who would fall into the FPL range for expanded Medicaid will not qualify in their state, and will not earn enough to qualify for premium subsidies.[59] The current rules for Medicaid coverage are complex and vary by state, with states imposing both income and asset tests on applicants. Additionally, eligibility criteria can vary widely based on which qualification group a person belongs to.

So, how will the gap affect seniors? Individuals who elected early retirement prior to age 65 are not eligible for Medicare. Instead,

58 The Henry J. Kaiser Family Foundation, "Status of State Action on Medicaid Expansion Decision, as of July 1, 2013," http://kff.org/medicaid/state-indicator/state-activity-around-expanding-medicaid-under-the-affordable-care-act/#map, Aug 23, 2013.
59 Ricardo Alonso-Zaldivar, "Medicaid Coverage Gap Looms," The Columbus Dispatch, http://www.dispatch.com/content/stories/national_world/2013/07/02/medicaid-coverage-gap-looms.html, October 22, 2013.

they must find insurance on the private market. This places early retirees in the pool of individuals who will be shopping for insurance in the exchanges under Obamacare. As we saw in the previous section, a couple that makes below $20,628 per year is not eligible for a subsidy in those exchanges.[60] Instead, it is assumed under Obamacare that low-income families will obtain health coverage through their state's Medicaid program under the Medicaid expansion. What the Obama administration did not count on was the Supreme Court's ruling that the Medicaid expansion was voluntary for the states. This has created a potential situation where these early retirees will be faced with no subsidy in the exchanges and an inability to qualify for Medicaid.

Under the current system, these retirees may not qualify for Medicaid, whether due to family status, health, assets, or income levels. Obamacare sought to change these policies by eliminating the asset tests for these individuals and moving to a strict, income-only test. Obamacare also created a new group of Medicaid-eligible individuals by expanding Medicaid eligibility to all individuals between ages 16 and 64. Using Ohio as an example of a state that has not adopted the Medicaid expansion, under current rules, a healthy couple with no children under age 19 is not eligible for coverage under any Medicaid program. If a family is in need of Medicaid, they are only eligible for coverage if family income is 90% of the FPL, which is significantly lower than the Obamacare limit of 133% of the FPL.[61]

Without Medicaid expansion, lower-income couples who retired early may be forced to continue working, simply due to the high costs of healthcare under Obamacare coupled with ineligibility for

60 Ibid., Figure 3.
61 Ohio Department of Job & Family Services, Office of Ohio Health Plans, "Ohio Medicaid Eligibility Guidelines," http://jfs.ohio.gov/OHP/consumers/docs/FPLs_general.pdf, Apr 9, 2008

subsidies due to low income. As of January 2013, only nine states provide full coverage for non-senior adults without children under Medicaid.[62] The existence and size of the coverage gap varies by state, but it is something that will be felt in all states that do not accept Medicaid expansion.

OUR VIEW: We believe that many small employers will drop their employee healthcare insurance coverage since Obamacare will supplement or even pay for the employees' insurance premiums. Most small business employees will receive better healthcare insurance under Obamacare as well as financial support to pay the premiums through the premium assistance provisions of Obamacare. Business owners may then choose to use funds they would have paid for healthcare insurance for their employees to provide other non-medical benefits, or they may choose to opt out altogether. Small business owners are likely to see Obamacare as a way out of paying for employee healthcare costs that provide less-perceived value by their employees. These employees normally are unaware of the cost of the benefits being paid on their behalf and the impact that these dramatically escalating benefit costs have on the bottom line of the business.

LIMITS ON COVERAGE

So far, we have looked at the two most significant parts of Obamacare that will impact individuals: the carrot and stick of premium assistance and penalties. However, it is also important to

---

62 Kaiser Commission on Medicaid and Uninsured, "Getting into Gear for 2014: Findings from a 50-State Survey of Eligibility, Enrollment, Renewal, and Cost-Sharing Policies in Medicaid and CHIP, 2012-2013," http://kaiserfamilyfoundation.files.wordpress.com/2013/05/8401.pdf, Jan 2013, 2.

look at a surprising unintended victim of Obamacare: high-dollar health plans. The law contains a hidden tax on so-called "Cadillac" health plans, which were sold to the American people as a tax on the health plans of high-powered executives. The *New York Times* has reported that this provision of Obamacare will have a drastic impact on both public- and private-sector labor unions, both traditional Democratic allies.

What most Americans did not know was that Obamacare would have the biggest impact on regular, hard-working Americans such as teachers, first responders, or factory workers with union contracts. Over the past few years, unions negotiated increases in health benefits in place of monetary compensation. This was a win-win for both employers and employees, who benefited from the preferential tax treatment of health benefits. These benefits are now in jeopardy.

Under Obamacare, employers providing sponsored plans with premium costs above a certain threshold will face taxes on these benefits. Many of these plans qualify as "Cadillac" plans, and even those that do not currently qualify will in the near future. This is because the definition of a "Cadillac" plans is not designed to keep up with the rising cost of healthcare. Over the past few years, the cost of healthcare has risen at a rate that exceeds the rate of inflation. In tough economic times, employers both public and private will be unable to pay the Obamacare penalties to maintain quality health insurance plans, pushing employees to lower cost coverage options. This means that quality health insurance plans, historically a staple of government and union jobs, could be on the way out.[63]

---

63 Kate Taylor, "Health Care Law Raises Pressure on Public Unions," New York Times, http://www.nytimes.com/2013/08/05/nyregion/health-care-law-raises-pressure-on-public-employees-unions.html?pagewanted=all, Aug 4, 2013.

> **OUR VIEW:** The penalties for union healthcare plans are just one example of an unintended consequence of Obamacare. Many of the unintended consequences of Obamacare have been addressed in this book, but what other effects of Obamacare are still unknown? Over the coming months and years as Obamacare takes effect, it will be important for consumers to work with professionals who are following developments in the law to make sure they plan for all possibilities.

Obamacare was intended to aid the uninsured in getting health coverage. It should be no surprise then that the result is that it will have a significant impact on working individuals. For individuals below retirement age who do not have employer-sponsored health coverage, Obamacare presents a choice: purchase health insurance or pay a penalty. In exchange for this choice, the government provides premium assistance and expands Medicaid for eligible individuals. For individuals who are under employer-sponsored health coverage, Obamacare may impact the type and quality of health insurance that employers are able to provide.

PART II:
OBAMACARE'S IMPACT AFTER RETIREMENT—THE COST OF AND ACCESS TO HEALTHCARE

As we discussed in Part I, Obamacare was designed to benefit Americans under the age of 65. However, even though it will not benefit seniors, it will have a large impact on the cost, availability, and quality of healthcare for seniors. This impact will be just as significant and far-reaching as the impact of the healthcare system for Americans under age 65.

In order to finance its expansion of the healthcare system for those under age 65, Obamacare cuts Medicare's budget by $45 billion per year over the next 10 years.[64] These cuts come primarily from a reduction in payment rates to providers and a reduction in payment rates to Medicare Advantage Plans. Even as other parts of Obamacare are delayed, there are no signs that there will be any delay in these spending cuts. The administration has attempted to downplay the effect of payment rates to providers for individual seniors, but it is easy to imagine what affect these cuts may have on hospitals and nursing homes. We could see decreased acceptance of Medicare by top providers who can afford to accept only patients with higher-paying private health insurance. This could lead to longer lines for a declining number of physicians who are overwhelmed by large patient loads.[65]

Impacts on Medicare Advantage Plans and Cost of Care

One of the significant ways in which Obamacare will impact seniors is through its adjustment to payments under Medicare Advantage Plans. Currently, Medicare is divided into parts A–D. Medicare Part A covers hospital stays, skilled nursing stays, home health, and hospice care. Medicare Part B covers physicians, outpatient and preventative services, and some home health benefits. Medicare Part D is a prescription drug benefit.[66] All three of these programs involve some form of cost-sharing or coinsurance

---

64 Tate, Obamacare Survival Guide, 137.
65 Ibid., 141–142.
66 One piece of good news out of Obamacare is the closing of the "donut hole." This refers to a gap in coverage under Medicare Part D in which seniors often faced significant out-of-pocket expenses for prescription drugs, being responsible for 100% of costs when drug spending reached $2,800 a year, until they reached $6,400 in drug spending. Under Obamacare, this is phased out gradually between now and 2020. Tate, Obamacare Survival Guide, 139.

between patients and Medicare.[67] Medicare Part C, also known as Medicare Advantage, was designed to aid low-income seniors in covering what Medicare would not cover, which can be up to 40% of the costs of healthcare.[68] Medicare Advantage Plans are provided through private insurers, and handle everything covered under Parts A, B, and generally D. These plans are distinct from Medicare supplements, which serve as secondary insurance to pick up costs that Medicare will not pay for, and are paid for in addition to regular Medicare A, B, and D premiums.

Individuals on the popular Medicare Advantage program (approximately 25% of Medicare recipients are enrolled in Advantage Plans) will see a direct reduction in the benefits they receive. While Obamacare is designed especially to aid low-income Americans under the age of 65 in obtaining health insurance, Obamacare directly harms low-income Americans over the age of 65 who utilize these plans. These reductions amount to around $308 less in payments *per person, per month*.[69] The total cuts to Advantage Plans over the next 10 years tops $130 billion.[70] These cuts could lead to increasing premiums, reduced coverage, or possibly a mass exodus of insurers altogether from the Medicare Advantage market.[71] This could mean disaster for seniors who depend on their Medicare Advantage Plan to absorb healthcare costs that Medicare will not pay for. These benefits can include dental, vision, or hearing coverage.[72]

The decline of Medicare Advantage Plans coupled with ever-increasing healthcare costs means that more of the burden of paying

---

67 The Henry J. Kaiser Family Foundation, "Medicare at a Glance," http://kff.org/medicare/fact-sheet/medicare-at-a-glance-fact-sheet/, Nov 14, 2012.

68 Tate, Obamacare Survival Guide, 143.

69 Rick Liuag, The Obamacare Bootcamp for Consultants Handbook, 18.

70 Tate, Obamacare Survival Guide, 144.

71 Ibid., 144.

72 Centers for Medicare & Medicaid Services, "CMS Product No. 11474," http://www.medicare.gov/Pubs/pdf/11474.pdf, Oct 2010.

for necessary medical care will fall directly on the pocketbooks of seniors rather than insurers. Seniors need to be prepared and plan for these increasing costs in the future.

ACCESS TO CARE

The final and perhaps most significant impact Obamacare will have on seniors is on access to care. As discussed in the introduction to this section, Obamacare imposed drastic cuts on Medicare spending over the next 10 years. This combined with the changes outlined in Part I of this chapter creates a perfect storm that will severely inhibit the ability of seniors to get private healthcare. To conclude, we will look at how the Medicare rules work against seniors and limit the care options available to seniors outside of Medicare.

With billions of dollars in Medicare cuts lined up, many providers will be seeking higher reimbursement rates. While in the past it may have been difficult to find new patients, these cuts are timed perfectly to coincide with a massive influx of new consumers into the healthcare marketplace: the previously uninsured. In 2010, around 50 million Americans were without health insurance.[73] Some of those uninsured will choose to pay the penalty rather than sign up for health insurance, but millions are expected to sign up for coverage through the new exchanges. Many of these will be individuals in dire need of healthcare, who were previously uninsurable due to pre-existing conditions.[74]

These individuals, along with many healthy individuals who would otherwise have avoided the doctor, will provide a new revenue stream for providers. These new patients will provide an attractive

73 Tate, Obamacare Survival Guide, 53.
74 Ibid., 57.

alternative to Medicare and Medicaid patients who a doctor may have previously cared for, due to the higher reimbursement rates of Obamacare. It would be unsurprising to see many providers stop accepting Medicare patients to focus on caring for new patients with insurance through the exchanges.

This will leave Medicare patients facing longer waits at the doctor's office as physicians struggle to cope with the new demand for care. By 2015, the shortage of doctors could be as high as 60,000.[75] This will make it harder to get care that is necessary. Declining reimbursement rates may mean that top doctors exit the Medicare coverage field altogether, meaning lower-quality service for seniors. The end result is that seniors will be faced with higher costs, longer waits, and lower-quality coverage under Medicare.

The impact of Obamacare will be far reaching on all Americans. This is especially true for seniors, who will be faced with rising healthcare costs, decreasing Medicare benefits, declining quality of care, and a shortage of physicians. It will be vital in the coming years that seniors develop a plan to cope with these challenges.

> **OUR VIEW:** Planning for medical costs in retirement will become extremely important in the coming years, as the highest-quality care may no longer be available to Medicare patients. Higher-quality care may be available to those who have planned and can pay out-of-pocket for their medical expenses. Even if you have the desire to pay privately for your healthcare, you may not have that option if you are on Medicare. This will be discussed in more detail in Chapter 6.

---

75 Liuag, Obamacare Bootcamp for Consultants, 14

The Takeaway: How Obamacare Will Affect Seniors

- Every individual must get health insurance or pay an income-based penalty.

- Seniors with low income who are not eligible for Medicare may be forced onto Medicaid or fall into a gap where they will receive neither Medicare nor Medicaid if they are in a state that does not participate in the Obamacare-expanded Medicaid program.

- Medicare Advantage Plans will be targeted heavily and may be a thing of the past.

- Obamacare is not designed for seniors and will be detrimental to their ability to afford and access care.

Section 1:
How Will I Afford Care?

"When I was young I thought that money was the most important thing in life; now that I am old I know that it is."

—Oscar Wilde

Chapter 3:

Saving, Protecting, and Insuring Through Obamacare

As both the cost of care and your ability to access it become a larger and larger burden, the question becomes: Where will you find the money to afford the healthcare you and your spouse will require and to provide income when pensions are reduced? It stands to reason that in the not-too-distant future, quality healthcare provided by a professional you can trust will come at a premium. Will you be able to afford that premium?

This chapter will focus on several ways to ensure that you will be able to answer these questions in the affirmative and be able to enjoy the retirement you had planned. We will show that post-Obamacare, every retiree will need to plan (1) to shelter the assets they have from new taxes, (2) to protect their assets from increasingly aggressive government programs such as Medicaid Estate Recovery, and (3) to create protected funds that will allow them to afford the care they need for themselves and their spouse.

We will explore the new taxes that will be imposed under Obamacare as well as highlight the need to revise your existing estate and trust planning to ensure that it is up-to-date and that it maximizes tax savings for your family, avoiding the newly developed tax traps. We will also focus on the need to increase your protection from the growing list of liabilities and rising healthcare costs by insulating your hard-earned assets in protected trusts and accounts.

PART I:
SAVING YOUR MONEY THROUGH MINIMIZING TAXES

THE DEATH OF THE DEATH TAX AND REBIRTH OF THE CAPITAL GAINS TAX

The federal estate tax exemption was raised to $5.25 million dollars and will be increased to adjust for inflation each year. The tax rate was reduced to 40% of the excess. Effective January 1, 2013, the Ohio estate tax was repealed. While estate tax laws have relaxed to a degree, capital gains and income tax rates have tightened, increasing nearly 58% from 2012.

Figure 3–A below illustrates the changes to the capital gains tax rates for 2013. Beginning in 2013, the federal capital gains tax rate was increased to 20%. In addition to the tax in the table below, states have also increased their version of the tax, with Ohio currently around 6.5%. Effectively, the tax on gains between federal and state is now nearly 30%, and more increases are on the horizon.

Figure 3–A: Snapshot of 2013 Federal Capital Gain Tax Rate[76]

Single Taxpayer	Married Filing Jointly	Capital Gain Tax Rate	Section 1411 Medicare Surtax	Combined Tax Rate
$0–$36,250	$0–$72,500	0%	0%	0%
$36,250–$200,000	$72,500 - $250,000	15%	0%	15%
$200,000–$400,000	$250,000 - $450,000	15%	3.8%	18.8%
$400,001 +	$450,001 +	20%	3.8%	23.8%

---

76 "New 3.8% Medicare Surtax and 20% Capital Gain Tax," Asset Preservation Inc., http://apiexchange.com/index_main.php?id=8&idz=236

The Affordable Care Act, or ACA, has instituted an additional 3.8% surtax on all investment income. This tax applies to individual Americans with adjusted gross income greater than $200,000 and couples with adjusted gross income in excess of $250,000. The IRS recently published 159 pages of rules implementing this surtax. It applies to a wide range of investments, from stocks and bonds, commodity securities and derivatives, to trusts and annuities as well as individual securities traders.

The new regulations also include a 0.9% healthcare tax on wages for individuals in the same income bracket. Additionally, as Figure 3–B below indicates, the Affordable Care Act is riddled with over 20 hidden taxes and fees, many relating to capital gains or investment income targeting the "top" income earners. The goal of these taxes and the increase to capital gains is to raise more than $317.2 billion over the next 10 years to pay for the nearly $1 trillion healthcare law.

Figure 3–B: New Taxes Associated with the Affordable Care Act [77]

Provision	March 2010 Estimate, 2010-2019, Billion US$	June-July 2012 Re-Estimate, 2013-2022, Billion US$
Additional 0.9% payroll tax on wages and self-employment income and new 3.8% tax on dividends, capital gains, and other investment income for taxpayers earning over $200,000 (singles) / $250,000 (married)	210.2	317.7
"Cadillac" tax on high-cost plans*	32	111
Employer mandate*	52	106
Annual tax on health insurance providers*	60.1	101.7
Individual mandate*	17	55
Annual tax on drug manufacturers/importers*	27	34.2
2.3% excise tax on medical device manufacturers/importers*	20	29.1
Limit Flexible Spending Accounts in cafeteria plans*	13	24
Raise 7.5% AGI floor on medical expense deduction to 10%*	15.2	18.7
Deny eligibility of "black liquor" for cellulosic biofuel producer credit	23.6	15.5
Codify economic substance doctrine	4.5	5.3
Increase penalty for non-qualified HSA distributions*	1.4	4.5
Impose limitations on the use of HSAs, FSAs, HRAs, and Archer MSAs to purchase over-the-	5.0	4
Impose fee on insured and self-insured health plans; patient-centered outcomes research trust	2.6	3.8
Eliminate deduction for expenses allocable to Medicare Part D subsidy	4.5	3.1
Impose 10% tax on tanning services*	2.7	1.5
Limit deduction for compensation to officers, employees, directors, and service providers of	0.6	0.8
Modify section 833 treatment of certain health organizations	0.4	0.4
Other revenue effects	60.3	222
Total Gross Tax Increase:	**569.2**	**1,058.3**

* Provision targets households earning less than $250,000.

---

77 Joint Committee on Taxation Estimates, prepared by Ways and Means Committee Staff

The Beginning of an Era of Outdated Estate Planning Strategies

January 2013 was the beginning of a new era in estate and trust planning. Major changes to tax laws on both the federal and state levels have caused a dramatic shift in the purpose of such planning. Accordingly, many trusts and estate plans that were drafted prior to 2013 have become outdated, and in some cases, obsolete. If not fixed, these outdated plans can create dangerous tax traps. These tax traps can cost you valuable funds that you may need to afford quality healthcare in the future.

Many of these changes have resulted from changes to the estate tax. The estate tax is based on the size of your estate at the time of death. Estate taxes are paid from the estate before distributions are made to the beneficiaries. Last year the estate tax rate in Ohio was 6% on the excess up to $500,000 and 7% above that. The federal estate tax was 55% of the excess above $5,120,000. Under the old law, the goal was to *exclude* assets from your estate at the time of death to avoid estate tax. However, one of the drawbacks of excluding assets from your estate, other than the obvious lack of control, is that your family can lose out on major capital gains tax savings.

Capital gains tax applies to the sale of assets that appreciate in value over time, such as real estate, stocks, or other investments. It is a tax on the appreciation in value between the time you purchase and the time you sell. It centers upon an accounting concept known as "cost basis," which is essentially the price you pay for the asset. Gain is calculated by subtracting the basis from the sale price.

> *Example*: You buy land in Ohio for $200,000. You sell it for $250,000. You have a $50,000 capital gain. In Ohio, this is

taxed at roughly between 20%-30% (including both state and federal) resulting in $10,000-$15,000 of profit lost to taxes.

The Value of "Basis Step-up"

Going along with the concept of basis is a hidden benefit in the tax code called "basis step-up." Basis step-up occurs when you die and pass appreciated assets on to your family—instead of the basis being what you paid for it, the basis "steps up" to the current market value. The result is that if they sell the asset for the market value, they have no taxable gain.

Example: You buy land in Ohio for $200,000. You sell it for $250,000. You have a $50,000 capital gain. In Ohio, this is taxed at roughly between 20%–30% (including both state and federal) resulting in $10,000–$15,000 of profit lost to taxes.

The Old AB Trust Strategy

The only way to ensure that your spouse or family can get the benefit of step-up in basis is by *including* assets in your estate at death. However prior to 2013, the goal of estate planning was exactly the opposite: to exclude assets from your estate as a trade-off for not paying the onerous federal estate tax. For example, as shown in Figure 3–C, the old classic "AB Trust" divided assets within the trust into separate shares (share "A" and share "B") at the death of the first spouse. The strategy here was to ensure that the deceased spouse's share of the estate, what became "Trust B," was not to be included in the survivor's share held in "Trust A." The result was that only "Trust A" was subject to the estate tax at the death of the second spouse, effectively sheltering half of the estate from estate tax.

Figure 3–C: Structure of AB Trusts

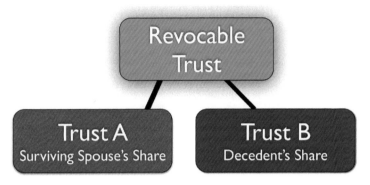

Before 2013, in a world where combined state and federal estate tax rates could be as high as 62%, excluding assets from your estate made sense. **Simply put, under the old laws the estate tax posed a much larger threat than the capital gains tax**. The drawback to the old classic "AB" plan, rarely explained to most families, is that because Trust B is not included in the surviving spouse's estate, Trust B does not get a new step-up in basis at the surviving spouse's death. This means that the heirs will pay capital gains tax on the difference in the value of Trust B's assets from the first to second death. However, with recent changes in estate tax laws described later in this section, the estate tax is no longer the biggest threat. As a result, the classic AB Trust has become obsolete for most families. Not only does it create an unnecessary division, increased administration costs, and a limitation on the survivor's ability to use trust assets, it also creates capital gains tax traps that can be very costly to both the surviving spouse and the family.

> **OUR VIEW:** It is important to have a trust that builds in flexibility if laws or circumstances change in the future. Traditionally, trusts have been rigid documents and were not flexible enough to accommodate changes in the law or other shifts in personal circumstances over time. The

traditional AB Trust is normally no longer a necessary or desirable tool because it forces a split of the estate at the death of the first spouse. Under current estate tax laws, this split creates adverse tax consequences and unnecessary hassles for the survivor.

Direct Gifting to Avoid Estate Tax

The other "classic" strategy to exclude assets from the estate was to give them away prior to death. Generally, assets that were properly gifted prior to death were not includable in the decedent's estate.[78] In instances where the gift was cash, this was an effective way to reduce estate tax exposure. However, when the gifts were comprised of appreciated assets, such as land, stock, or investments, these gifts created a huge tax trap for the recipient of the gift.

The IRS rules allow basis step-up at death. But when assets are gifted during life, the rule is just the opposite. The owner's basis carries over to the recipient of the gift. For example, let's say you purchased land 50 years ago for $100,000 and the market value of that property is now $1,000,000. To shelter that $1,000,000 asset from estate taxes, you give it to your son. IRS rules dictate that your basis of $100,000 carries over to your son. If he ever decides to sell the property, he will owe capital gains tax on the $900,000 gain. That equates to nearly $270,000 lost to taxes (see Figure 3–D).

---

78 Gifts are added back into the estate for federal and state estate tax purposes, but there are ways to get around that restriction by using the annual exclusion or the use of the discount, which are beyond the scope of this discussion.

Figure 3–D: Capital Gains Tax on Assets Gifted during Life

$1,000,000 Sale Price - $100,000 Basis = $900,000 Gain
x 30% Tax Rate
$270,000 TAX DUE

Had you left the land in your estate until your death, your son would have received a full step-up to the value at the date of death, thus eliminating the capital gains tax burden. However, prior to 2013, your estate would have paid state and federal estate tax on the land, which would have resulted in a 62% tax or $620,000 on that same million-dollar tract (see Figure 3–E).

Figure 3–E: Estate Tax on Assets in the Estate at Death

$1,000,000 x 55% Federal Estate Tax = $550,000
$1,000,000 x 7% Ohio Estate Tax = $70,000
$620,000 TOTAL ESTATE TAX DUE

This is a clear illustration of how the estate tax posed a far greater threat than capital gains tax. For decades, estate and trust planning focused on reducing estate tax at the expense of capital gains consequences. However, this landscape has changed markedly following the tax law changes in 2013.

HOW TO RESTRUCTURE YOUR EXISTING LIVING TRUST TO SAVE THOUSANDS IN CAPITAL GAINS TAXES

IRS rules regarding step-up in basis are, as expected, very tricky, and planning for them effectively requires the use of special trusts and other planning methods. As discussed above, the traditional

AB Trust is usually not appropriate in today's tax environment. Today's tax environment requires a very sophisticated trust that is designed to provide both protection and flexibility. The modern revocable trust includes two new components that old trusts did not have. The first of these components allows the surviving spouse to have options. Instead of mandating the AB split at the death of the first spouse, the split is optional, allowing the surviving spouse to evaluate the best strategy to take depending on the tax laws and the size of the estate at the time of the first spouse's death. One of the greatest difficulties of trust planning is being rigid enough to meet the client's needs but flexible enough to withstand future changes in the law. An average client establishes a trust in their early 50s. It is rare that the tax laws and the size of their estate remain consistent over the next 20 to 30 years of their life. To draft a trust that locks in decisions that will be made 20 years in the future is not only unrealistic but also impractical. Giving the surviving spouse options within the trust provides flexibility for future changes in the law. This way, if estate tax laws become more strict and it makes sense to split the trust, the surviving spouse can choose to do that. However, if the current trend remains the same and capital gains tax remains the dominant threat, a second component can be implemented to maximize tax savings.

This second component is using a "tax basis bridge." This strategy is designed to harness the full power of the basis step-up rules for the benefit of the surviving spouse. The tax basis bridge causes the entire trust, not simply the decedent's half, to receive a full step-up in basis. Should the surviving spouse choose to sell appreciated assets, he or she can do so without the burden of capital gains tax. On the other hand, should the surviving spouse choose to keep the assets, the children will receive a full basis step-up on all assets at his or her death.

A trust that contains both spousal options and a tax basis bridge allows for maximum tax savings and maximum flexibility for the almost certain tax law changes of the future. With both of these components, a couple can ensure that they are well prepared to lose as little as possible to taxes and to keep as much as possible in the hands of their family. This modern trust also ensures that family assets will not have to be unnecessarily sold to pay taxes and gives the heirs significant tax benefits.

How to Rescue Your Old "B Trust" to Provide Flexibility to the Surviving Spouse and Save Capital Gains Taxes

Revising an existing AB Trust to allow flexibility and to take advantage of current tax laws is a logical option when both spouses are still living. However, when one spouse has died and the estate has already been split into the "B Trust," the situation is much different. The biggest disadvantage of the AB Trust is that the cost basis of all assets allocated to the B Trust is locked at the value of those assets at the first spouse's date of death. The property will continue to appreciate during the life of the surviving spouse, but at his or her death, the heirs receive only a step-up in basis on the surviving spouse's half of the trust. The portion that is in the B Trust does not receive another step-up—the value is locked in at the time of the first spouse's death. The result is that the heirs will be trapped into paying capital gains tax on the appreciation in the B Trust. In addition, assets locked in a B Trust are vulnerable to a nursing home spenddown and may be lost completely if the surviving spouse experiences a catastrophic healthcare situation.

However, the certainty of this capital gains tax can be avoided through the implementation of a technique known as the "B-Trust

Rescue." This is a method used to revise an existing B Trust so that it will be included in the survivor's estate at death. As a result, the entire trust estate will receive a step-up in basis at second death, thereby reducing the tax impact on the heirs. If you have the B Trust problem we just described, you should take immediate steps to seek legal advice, as the tax savings may be hundreds of thousands of dollars.

It is clear that capital gains has become the new tax trap, in addition to the many hidden taxes and surcharges within the Affordable Care Act. Therefore, the goal of effective trust planning is now based on how to include assets into your estate while protecting them from these increasing taxes and charges. By including assets, you can take full advantage of the step-up rules and greatly minimize the capital gains tax your spouse and family may pay. By saving on taxes, more funds become available to obtain the quality care you and your family expect.

There is no doubt that changes are required to ensure that you can take advantage of the hidden benefits built into the tax code and avoid the traps and potholes. However, taxes are only one of a whole host of new threats to your assets. Modern asset protection often involves using not just one trust, but multiple trusts working together to mitigate these threats. **The question in future estate planning will no longer be which trust is best to integrate your estate plan, but rather how to integrate several trusts into an estate plan to minimize taxation and provide asset protection for you and your children.**

OUR VIEW: Under Obamacare, seniors will need to be prepared to privately pay for more of their healthcare, and this will be expensive. As a senior, wouldn't you want the best medical treatment for your spouse, even if you had to pay for it? It is our belief that you must be prepared to take

> all possible tax savings and squirrel those savings away in protected funds or trusts to pay for the healthcare of you or your spouse when you need it—and you will probably need it!

PART II:
PROTECTING WHAT YOU HAVE ALREADY EARNED

WHAT YOU CAN DO TO AVOID MEDICAID ESTATE RECOVERY

In a time when healthcare costs are skyrocketing and government solutions only seem to make it worse, protecting your assets from the astronomical cost of healthcare is a very real and necessary precaution. Blindly relying on the government to cover your future healthcare costs is not a solution, since that reliance comes with a steep price tag. Remember, Obamacare is expanding Medicaid, and with the expansion of Medicaid comes the expansion of Medicaid Estate Recovery. Medicaid Estate Recovery is the program administered by the collections arm of the state's Attorney General's Office. They in turn hire private attorneys as "special counsel" who are empowered to go after the estate of anyone 55 years of age and older who has received Medicaid benefits. We have seen the state's collectors become more and more aggressive over the years. They will routinely place liens on family homes, farms, and business assets.

We represented a farmer whose family faced two liens that totaled over $400,000. The liens were placed against the family farm for Mom and Dad's nursing home bill that was paid by the state. The majority of the $400,000 lien was from Dad's nursing home bill, while Mom's lien was less than $20,000. Fortunately, we were able to prove Dad's lien was improperly placed and that, because of proper planning, the state actually had no legal claim against the farm. Unfortunately, not all families receive adequate representation. We firmly believe that if we had not represented the family, the state's special counsel/collection attorney would have liquidated the entire family farm without a legitimate claim and without remorse.

What this means to you is that you should not blindly trust the government. Instead, you should seek to achieve financial freedom by doing your own proper planning to protect your assets. Asset protection means protection not only from the cost of healthcare, but also from lawsuits, creditors, and unexpected catastrophic events. All of these liabilities can wipe out your assets in the blink of an eye. One bad event can cost you your life savings. Are you then willing to rely on the government to pay for your healthcare costs for the rest of your life? You will learn in later chapters how it is almost certain that cuts in Obamacare will require you to be responsible for more of your own medical care. Therefore, protecting your assets should be instinctual. You should not be ashamed of this instinctual feeling because protecting assets is the right thing to do for you and your family. As the Ohio Bar Association explained, asset protection is the legal reallocation of assets to reduce risk. It is not fraud.[79]

> **OUR VIEW:** It is not wrong to take legal steps to protect your hard-earned assets. What's wrong are government policies that routinely punish those who save and reward

79 "Report of the Estate Planning, Trust and Probate Law Section," Ohio Bar Association, https://www.ohiobar.org/General%20Resources/pubs/councilfiles/Report_of_the_Estate_Planning_Trust_and_Probate_Law_Section_11_10.pdf

those who do not. Remember, the laws are not always set up to benefit you by default. Too often the default setting is set to benefit others. You should not just accept these settings. Thankfully, we still have some laws that will favor those who save, but you do not get the benefit of these laws automatically. You should cherry-pick those laws that work for you and opt out of those laws that do not.

People will move their financial assets from one type of investment to another to protect from the risk of loss in the market. Why not also move assets to reduce the risk of loss from bad things happening to you? For example, have you ever driven a neighbor's son to soccer practice? If you cause a terrible accident, who will be personally liable for your neighbor's son? Do you own a business? You may be surprised to find out that what your employees do can pass liability directly back to you. Maybe you are in a high-risk profession, as are doctors, financial advisors, lawyers, and rental property owners. Maybe you just own a lot of land, which equates to a lot of liability. All of these are reasons to protect assets even when you expect nothing bad to occur. Just remember, 46,000 new attorneys graduated in 2012, and every year more than 40,000 will continue to graduate.[80] There are not enough jobs out there for these attorneys but yet all of them have the license to sue. So even when you do everything right, you can still be subject to being hit with a frivolous lawsuit.

Fortunately for Ohioans, we have more options than most states. The law allows us to protect our assets from these liabilities. Trusts can be set up to protect from some or all of the liabilities mentioned above. **However, the law requires that you protect assets well before you expect things to go south. If you wait until something happens, it is usually too late to protect your assets!**

---

80 Ibid.

Insurance and LLCs—Not Good Enough

Getting insurance is usually the first step to take when protecting your assets. However, insurance may not be enough. Insurance companies are there to make money, not to pay claims. So although they will pay claims, your claim had better be airtight. If it's not covered under the policy, you're not getting paid. Perhaps the Ohio Bar Association best summarizes the issue.

> "We live in a litigious society and adequate insurance may not be reasonably obtained at an affordable price to protect an insured from most claims. Some claims will exceed the available limits, in other cases coverage may be denied or the insurance company might fail."[81]

The Ohio Bar Association provides the classic example of how insurance companies get out of paying a claim:

> "As an example: an executive was working from his home one weekend and had a business delivery at his house. The UPS delivery person slipped on his son's skateboard and broke his back. The company insurance did not cover the accident, because it occurred off business premises. Both the homeowner's insurance and the executive's umbrella insurance policy declined coverage because it was a business delivery. Instead, the executive was personally liable for the entire judgment amount."[82]

Even when insurance companies pay, there are maximum limits to how much they will pay. With multi-million dollar judgments passed by juries these days, no maximum limit can guarantee complete security.

---

81 Ibid
82 Ibid

Historically, creating a Limited Liability Company (LLC) was the traditional method of protecting assets for business owners. However, even these powerful tools are not enough. First, many misunderstand the protection that LLCs provide. They limit the liability of your company to your company. So they don't actually protect the assets in the LLC. The LLC is protecting your assets *outside* of the LLC from the liabilities of the company. But, if you are found to be personally liable, then the LLC then provides very little protection. Finding the owner as personally liable for the liability of the company is a legal term called "piercing the veil." Piercing the veil of protection means that you, as the owner, acted negligently or intentionally, and therefore the claim against the company should attach to your personal assets as well.

Furthermore, an LLC does not protect your company from your own personal liability that is unrelated to your business. For example, if you have a very large hospital bill to pay, the hospital's collections attorney will go after your interest and right to receive distributions from your LLC. Even though the debt is completely unrelated to your company, a judge in Ohio would allow the creditor to garnish your rights to the LLC income because your personal liabilities, which include your healthcare expenses, are not barred by the LLC structure.

DIRECT GIFTING IS A BAD IDEA

Although having insurance or creating some protection with LLCs may not be enough, please do not solve the problem by simply transferring assets to your children or other family members. Gifting assets directly usually creates more problems than it solves. For example, in order to avoid the cost of your healthcare from affecting your home, let's say you put your home in your children's names. Believe it or not, people do this because they say they trust their children, but trusting your child is not the only issue. What people do not realize is that by transferring their home in their children's names, they have just attached all of their children's potential liabilities to their home. What if one of the children gets a divorce? What if one them has a car accident or a healthcare cost that they cannot afford? Your home is now titled to your children and therefore available to all of their liabilities and their creditors. Therefore, transferring your home directly to another can be a very bad idea. In addition, from a tax point of view, transferring appreciated assets such as real estate or securities directly to your children can be devastating due to the law of basis step-up as explained in the previous section. This can cost your children thousands of dollars in unnecessary capital gains tax.

THE RIGHT IDEA

Using special trusts to protect assets is a better idea because these trusts can be created so that the owner of the asset is the trust, and not the children or anyone else. Why would you want a trust to own your asset and not you or another person? "People" come with inherent liabilities. A trust can't get sick and incur hospital bills. A trust can't cause a car accident and a trust can't file for a divorce.

Combining insurance, LLCs, and trusts is what is needed to achieve real well-rounded protection. However, not every trust does the same thing. Not all trusts provide protection. In fact, most trusts will avoid probate and maybe, if you're lucky, have some tax savings provisions, but most will lack the asset protection element. The majority of trusts are termed "revocable living trusts" and these trusts provide little or no asset protection. Other irrevocable trusts will provide protection, but the protection will be in exchange for the complete loss of control.

A good asset protection trust should be designed specifically for your needs in order to provide protection and to also give an element of control to the person creating the trust. A good asset protection trust should also be a trust that does not require the trustee to make additional tax filings every year. A good trust should be set up to be tax-neutral, so it does not change the taxable status of the asset from the tax treatment prior to transferring the asset into the new trust. A trust should not require more taxes to be paid nor require any more reporting to the government than is already necessary. Further, a trust with a separate tax identification number is generally taxed at a higher rate. These trusts are called non-grantor trusts. To discourage the wide use of these trusts, the tax brackets are significantly condensed, meaning a trust will hit the highest tax bracket after only a very small amount of income, as shown in Figure 3–F.

Figure 3–F: 2013 Trust Tax Rate Table [83]

Trust's Taxable Income	Tax Owed
< $2,450	15% of the taxable income
$2,450–$5,700	$367.50 plus 25% of the excess over $2,450
$5,700–$8,750	$1,180 plus 28% of the excess over $5,700
$8,750–$11,950	$2,034 plus 33% of the excess over $8,750
> $11,950	$3,090 plus 39.6% of the excess over $11,950

83 "Rev. Proc. 2013-15 of the American Taxpayer Relief Act," Internal Revenue Service Publication, http://www.irs.gov/pub/irs-drop/rp-13-15.pdf

At just $11,951 in income, a trust will be taxed at the new highest tax bracket of 39.6%. Add in Ohio's income tax of 6% (2013) and the 3.8% Obamacare surtax on investments, and you are looking at roughly half of the trust income going to taxes. Therefore, when possible, asset-protected trusts should be created under the Social Security number of the creator of the trust. These trusts are called "Grantor Trusts" because they are taxed to the person who created the trust and granted the asset to the trust. These trusts are taxed to the person as if the trust did not exist, thereby getting all of the benefits of the protected trust without the negative tax implication of a higher income tax rate.

> **OUR VIEW**: In order to preserve your wealth to provide for your future medical needs and ensure a maximum wealth transfer to your heirs, you need a plan—a plan that is specifically tailored to your needs based upon a specific analysis of your income, assets, family relationships and the current health status of you and your spouse. This plan will normally consist of several trusts, LLCs, and other legal or financial structures or products to specifically meet your needs. Just like an old watch that needed several gears to make it tell the correct time, your plan must have the "right gears" to enable you and your spouse to obtain the medical care that you will require to live long and healthful lives and not become a burden to your children.

PART III:
INSURING AND SELF-INSURING BY INTEGRATING LEGAL AND FINANCIAL PRODUCTS THAT PROVIDE PROTECTED FUNDS

What can you do with the protected trust assets? You can pair the protected trusts with financial products (such as life insurance, long-term care insurance, and fixed or indexed investments) that will allow for growth without the risk of all liabilities mentioned in Parts I and II of this chapter. This will guarantee that, should you need access to the funds in the future for your care, the funds will be there.

For example, if you are not a risk-taker, you can purchase an investment that is guaranteed to grow when the market goes up but not go down when the market goes down. These are called indexed investments. They allow the investor to gain from the upside of the market but never take a loss on the downside. Of course the gain from the upside of a market swing is not as much as if you were really playing the market, but, if security is your goal, playing the market is not always a good thing. If you are more comfortable with risk, you can invest in securities, but it is our view that these securities should normally be protected by special trusts. Since the funds are in the protected trusts, they are also protected from your personal liabilities and are available to pay for future healthcare expenses.

In addition, if these funds are properly structured, they will not be subject to government medical spenddowns. If you do choose to use these protected funds, you also get to choose what medical procedure you find necessary, versus only being limited to what the government says is and is not necessary. A protected fund of this type keeps you in control and gives you what all asset-protection planners desire: financial freedom. You can also stand proud knowing that you have a self-made safety net for your family—one that you created, and one that does not rely on the government.

Should you choose to not use all of these funds, the protection can be passed on to your spouse and children. With all the buzz about cliffs and debt ceilings, you should know by now that your children's generation will be able to rely on the government for benefits even less than your generation can now. The benefits that will be provided will continue to be unfairly provided in a way that penalizes people who save. In other words, a child who spends his or her inheritance will perhaps qualify for a public benefit down the road, but a child who does the right thing and saves his or her inheritance will not qualify for any help from the government.

Therefore, a protected inheritance is desirable because the inheritance will fall outside of the purview of government programs that penalize those with assets. The protected inheritance will not be considered an asset owned by the child because it will continue to be owned by the trust. So even for those children who are successful themselves, parents who wish to leave an inheritance for their children should think about taking it one step further by providing them a protected inheritance.

The same applies for parents who have children with special needs. The Affordable Care Act will allow special needs children to obtain health insurance since existing conditions can no longer be a factor. However, private health insurance will not always prevent the need for other public benefits, like income from Supplemental Security Income (SSI) and even Medicaid, since private health insurance will not cover close to what Medicaid currently covers. Trusts should still be created by parents so that the inheritance they leave to their special needs child can be used for their benefit but not disqualify them from additional help.

However, regardless of whether or not your children are disabled, have special needs, or are financially sound, you should still leave them a protected inheritance because you should provide them with the same financial freedom you want to have yourself. Giving them the same choices when it comes to healthcare is a wonderful gift to your children, a gift that they will appreciate for the rest of their lives.

THE TAKEAWAY:
PREPARING YOUR ASSETS FOR OBAMACARE

- Under Obamacare seniors will be responsible for paying for more of their own care, and therefore cannot afford to lose it to taxes that can be avoided.

- The 2013 changes to the tax laws have changed the fundamental goals of estate planning. Seniors who did their planning before 2013 should have it reviewed in order to ensure that they do not pay taxes unnecessarily.

- Increasingly aggressive government programs, such as the Medicaid Estate Recovery Program, have made it necessary to utilize asset protection strategies, such as trusts, to protect assets from the liens that these programs impose on homes, farms, and family businesses.

- Utilizing the traditional methods of protecting business owners' assets, such as creating LLCs, is no longer good enough to ensure protection of non-business assets. Instead, business owners should seek a well-rounded strategy that integrates insurance, LLCs, and trusts.

Chapter 4:
Using Longevity Planning to Establish a Perpetual Healthcare Safety Net

"The question isn't at what age I want to retire, it's at what income."

—George Foreman

Every tsunami can be traced back to one event, such as an earthquake, which causes a chain reaction that results in the massive waves. The same concept—an event that causes a series of chain reactions—can be found for each of the great waves that are about to hit baby boomers. No wave is the causing event more clearly than the first wave, the failure of government programs and public pension systems, and that causing event was that these programs were not established with a proper understanding of the future risk of longevity. This miscalculation then caused a chain reaction, which was the rather surprising trend that as life expectancy rose, the age of retirement stayed relatively steady. This resulted in longer retirements. This in turn caused another chain reaction, which was that seniors financed these longer retirements with income from programs that were already strained because they were not being designed for the mere increase in life expectancy.

Decades of this occurring has led to the meltdown that the government and public pension systems are currently experiencing. Given the recent distress signals that are being issued from these programs, such as Social Security claiming it will be completely broke by 2033 or public pensions systems seeking bankruptcy or pension reforms, it is clear that the government has learned its lesson on underestimating the effects of longevity.[84] The question then becomes, will baby boomers learn from these lessons, or will they experience results similar to those of the government programs?

The good news is that when longevity planning is taken into account from the beginning of retirement, it can not only be used to avoid tremendous pitfalls, but also to provide a safety net for seniors by providing something that should be a concern to every baby boomer already: how they will finance healthcare. As is explored throughout this book, Obamacare is not designed for seniors. In fact, quite the opposite is true, as evidenced by the fact that most significant change to care for seniors under the Affordable Care Act was Medicare reimbursement cuts. There are two solutions to cope with these problems: (1) maximizing and protecting assets, as discussed in the previous chapter, and (2) **implementing a longevity plan to optimize income, as described below**.

"Longevity planning" is getting more income through the use of Social Security and pension-claiming strategies as well as tax rules, which get you more income for a longer period of time. This chapter will discuss how to incorporate longevity planning into estate and healthcare planning. Part I will explain the impact that longevity can have on healthcare and estate planning, why it poses such a risk, and how income is the cornerstone of constructing a longevity plan. Therefore, maximizing what is available from pensions is fundamental to longevity planning. Part II will discuss the strategies that can be used for private-sector employees,

---

84 "A Summary of the 2013 Annual Reports," Social Security and Medicare Boards of Trustees, http://www.ssa.gov/oact/trsum/

including tactics that can be used by private-sector couples, to maximize their Social Security benefit. Since the pension benefits that are available for private- and public-sector employees are different, private employees are able to receive Social Security, whereas public-sector, non-federal employees are excluded from Social Security. As such, longevity planning strategies for private-versus public-sector employees will be discussed separately. Lastly, Part III will conclude with a discussion of the extraordinarily difficult decision that is faced by public-sector employees who are seeking to claim benefits in light of widespread municipal bankruptcy and pension reform. This section will also explain the disadvantages that are faced by private/public-sector couples who are subjected to the claiming penalties of the Government Pension Offset Provision.

OUR VIEW: In the past most estate planning has focused on preserving and protecting a client's assets. Only recently have estate planners begun to listen to their clients and realize that an even greater concern for clients was the preservation and extension of income, which is known as "Longevity Planning." **The central concept in longevity planning is to make sure that neither you nor your spouse outlive your assets through unplanned overspending of income and then wind up trying to live the remainder of your life on what you might get from the government.** The consequences of failing to longevity plan may result in an unintended lifestyle of poverty and poor medical care with the burden of support being shifted to your children.

Our firm has recently reviewed and explored the longevity planning process. We have now developed computerized models using a combination of both legal and financial strategies to optimize and extend income. An example is included as Figure 4–B. This work was largely based on the conceptual work of Professor William Reichenstein of Baylor University in Texas. We would commend his publications including his book, *Social Security Strategies: How to Optimize Retirement Benefits*, for those who are more technically inclined.

PART I:
LONGEVITY PLANNING—HOW OPTIMIZING YOUR LIFETIME INCOME CAN DECREASE THE RISK OF LONGEVITY

One of the greatest factors that will affect the retirement planning of baby boomers is the risk of longevity. One of the biggest risks associated with longevity is that it is often overlooked or underestimated by retirees when planning for retirement. This oversight can cause fundamental flaws in even the most deliberate retirement planning—if you don't understand how long the term of your retirement might be, how can you possibly plan to financially support yourself through its duration? Therefore, the first step of longevity planning is to understand potential longevity and how it affects your healthcare and retirement planning.

UNDERSTANDING LONGEVITY: HAVE YOU BEEN WORKING OFF OF THE WRONG NUMBERS?

When the Social Security Act was passed in 1935, the average female life expectancy was 62, and for men it was only 58.[85] Almost 80 years later, life expectancy has increased by nearly 20 years and can only be expected to grow even more.[86] When considering life expectancy,

---

85 "Life Expectancy for Social Security," SSA, http://www.ssa.gov/history/lifeexpect.html, Aug 11, 2013.

a significant number of retirees might be making retirement-planning decisions based on the wrong statistical data, which is life expectancy from birth rather than life expectancy from retirement.[87] In 2011, the Center for Disease Control released that the average life expectancy from birth in the United States was 78.7 years.[88] However, this number is larger for an individual who actually lives to be old enough to retire, because that average no longer accounts for people who died before retirement. Social Security estimates that the current life expectancy for a man and woman turning 65 in 2013 is 84 and 86, respectively.[89]

Figure 4–A illustrates the drastic difference between the two estimates of life expectancy by showing the increase of life expectancy from retirement versus the increase in life expectancy from birth since Social Security's original enactment in 1936 to present day.

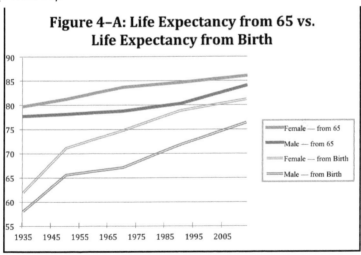

Figure 4–A: Life Expectancy from 65 vs. Life Expectancy from Birth

---

86 Arialdi M. Miniño and Sherry L. Murphey, "NCHS Data Brief No. 99: Death in the United States, 2010" U.S. Department of Health and Human Services (2012), http://www.cdc.gov/nchs/data/databriefs/db99.pdf, 1.

87 Ibid. In a recent survey, more than 40% of current retirees underestimated both their personal life expectancy and the average life expectancy from retirement by more than five years. Ibid.

88 Miniño and Murphy, "NCHS Data Brief No. 99," 1.

89 http://www.ssa.gov/planners/lifeexpectancy.htm

As shown, the difference between life expectancy from birth versus life expectancy from retirement is significant. Ultimately, the measure of life expectancy from 65 is the more realistic estimate of life expectancy for a person planning retirement and is the figure that should be used by baby boomer when planning for retirement. Failure to use the proper measure for the term of your retirement can have an insurmountable effect on your retirement planning.

How the Risk of Longevity Relates to Your Healthcare and Estate Planning

Longevity affects retirement planning because it is a fundamental determinant of the length of retirement. Only when considered in light of retirement planning can the risk of longevity be truly appreciated. A recent Gallup poll estimated that the average retirement age in the U.S. was 61 years old.[90] Consider a couple in which each spouse is around the same age and retires when they are 61. If they used the average life expectancy from birth, they will expect for their retirement to last until they are around 79 or for a term of 18 years. Conversely, if that same couple used the life expectancy from retirement, they will expect for their retirement to last until they are 86 or for a term of 25 years. **This difference of 7 years means that underestimating life expectancy leads to planning for only 72% of your retirement.** If you use the rule of thumb that some advisors recommend where you should expect to spend 80% of your pre-retirement salary in retirement,[91] this means that for a couple making $80,000 a year, the error in not planning for longevity has left you with a shortfall of nearly $450,000.

---

90 "Average Retirement Age," Gallup, http://www.gallup.com/poll/162560/average-retirement-age.aspx
91 "Estimate Your Retirement Income Needs," State Farm, http://www.statefarm.com/learning/life_stages/retire/estimate_needs.asp

Unfortunately for those who have not prepared properly, that is only half of the problem that is caused by underestimating longevity. The other half is healthcare planning. The risk of longevity is intricately linked with healthcare planning because living longer increases the likelihood that you will need more, and therefore spend more on, healthcare. The longer you live, the more you will need to access healthcare, and the more healthcare you need, the more money you will need to spend in order to get quality care. This is further intensified by Obamacare, which we believe will make affording care and obtaining access to care in retirement more expensive.

Further, increased longevity increases the possibility that someone "may decline cognitively and physically in later years," and therefore will require more care including long-term care.[92] If a retiree does in fact need long-term care, longevity may increase the time period over which the individual would have to pay for it out-of-pocket. When a retiree is subject to these expenses, unlike when the retiree was working, there is no way to replace those assets that were lost as a result of the expenses, except for income.

INCOME: THE CORNERSTONE OF LONGEVITY PLANNING

Properly planning for longevity is crucial because if an individual underestimates how long he or she will live, then it is likely that the individual's retirement was planned to be over an inaccurately short period of time.[93] **This short planning horizon can lead the individual to draw down retirement assets too quickly, increasing the likelihood that the individual will outlive personal**

---

92 "Society of Actuaries Key Findings and Issues: Longevity," Society of Actuaries (2012), http://www.soa.org/search.aspx?searchterm=longevity, 4.
93 Ibid., 6–12.

savings. This highlights the importance of income because, should the individual make this miscalculation, then income could serve as the primary way in which that individual can recover from this miscalculation and ultimately be able to self-sustain through the duration of retirement.

A retiree typically has two resources: assets that have been saved and income. Retirement income is composed of three sources: a public or private pension, government-sponsored programs, and income derived from personal savings or other assets. Unless the retiree begins working again or receives an inheritance, these pools of assets are mostly fixed at the time of retirement. Once fixed, these assets are subject to outside risks, the most significant of which is healthcare costs, which can cause assets to be completely depleted long before the death of the retiree.

A recent study illustrates the importance of income in maintaining your current lifestyle throughout the duration of your retirement.[94] This study categorized retirees into three income groups, from lowest to highest, and predicted the groups' risk of not being able to maintain that groups' current lifestyle over the course of retirement.[95] The retirees in the lowest income group were at more than a 70% risk of not being able to maintain the group's average standard of living.[96] However the risk decreased to 41.6% for those in the middle income group and was only 23.3% for retirees in the highest income group.[97]

That being said, in the light of Obamacare, maintaining the accustomed lifestyle is only one of many reasons why income is important in retirement. In an environment where it is advisable

94 Jack VanDerhei and Craig Copeland, "The EBRI Retirement Readiness Rating: Retirement Income Preparation and Future Prospects," Employee Benefit Research Institute (2010), http://www.ebri.org/pdf/briefspdf/EBRI_IB_07-2010_No344_RRR_RSPM1.pdf
95 Ibid.
96 Ibid., 24.
97 Ibid.

to put aside money to pay for healthcare expenses, income could be used to maintain or build those side funds, which could later be used to purchase healthcare. For example, income could be used to support your day-to-day expenses, and therefore allow you to maintain a separate fund that you could use for a healthcare emergency.

In addition, as baby boomers become impatient with the options that are being offered to them under Medicare, especially in light of the expected severe reductions of Medicare Advantage Plans, new insurance options could arise, and excess income could be the best way to afford the premiums. **As such, income provides baby boomers with something that is invaluable in the current unclear climate—options.**

PART II:
LONGEVITY PLANNING STRATEGIES FOR PRIVATE-SECTOR EMPLOYEES

For private-sector employees, maximizing Social Security benefits is the most important part of their longevity plan. Baby boomers are the beginning of a "pensionless generation," and private pensions are becoming exceedingly rare. As such, Social Security benefits are the most significant source of income for most baby boomers and, therefore, maximizing them is fundamental to longevity planning for private-sector employees. This part will explore the basics of Social Security benefits and how to maximize them.

The Basics of Claiming Social Security Benefits

Workers contribute to the Social Security system through payroll taxes on their earned income, which is enforced on the eligible employers under the authority of the Federal Insurance Contributions Act (FICA).[98] The amount that a worker contributes to Social Security varies depending on that worker's earnings record, and it is this record of contributions that is used to determine what is known as the Primary Insurance Amount (PIA).[99] **The PIA is computed by taking an adjusted average of the 35 highest years of the worker's contribution record prior to claiming.**[100] The PIA constitutes the base monthly benefit amount that individual is eligible to receive from Social Security.[101] However, the PIA is not the sole determinant of how much the individual will actually receive when a Social Security benefit is claimed. The amount that retirees receive varies depending on their age when they claim the benefit because Social Security imposes what is commonly referred to as actuarial adjustments.[102]

In order to encourage retirees to delay claiming Social Security benefits, Social Security both penalizes early claiming of Social Security benefits and rewards delayed claiming of Social Security benefits.[103] All claimants are assigned a Full

---

98 Federal State Reference Guide, IRS, Pub. 963, http://www.irs.gov/pub/irs-pdf/p963.pdf, 1-1 to -3, 3-1.

99 42 U.S.C. §§ 402(a), 415(a); Social Security Handbook, SSA, § 700 (July 30, 2007) http://www.socialsecurity.gov/OP_Home/handbook

100 42 U.S.C. § 415(a); "Your Retirement Benefit: How It Is Figured," SSA (2013), http://www.ssa.gov/pubs/10070.pdf. The exact method and intricacies of computing of the PIA are beyond the scope of this book, but for further explanation see Social Security Handbook (note 99), § 700.

101 42 U.S.C. § 402(a); Social Security Handbook, § 700.1.

102 42 U.S.C. § 402(q), (w); Gary Sidor, "Fact Sheet: The Social Security Retirement Age," Congressional Research Service (2013), http://www.fas.org/sgp/crs/misc/R41962.pdf, 2–4.

103 42 U.S.C. § 402(q), (w); see also Retirement Benefits, SSA, Pub. No. 05-10035 (2012), http://www.ssa.gov/pubs/10035.pdf, 5–8.

Retirement Age (FRA), which is determined by the individual's date of birth.[104] If the benefit is claimed at the individual's FRA, then the monthly benefit is exactly equal to the individual's PIA.[105] However, if claimed earlier or later then the individual's FRA, the amount of monthly benefits awarded is accordingly either penalized or awarded by receiving from a minimum of 70% up to a maximum of 132% of the individual's PIA.[106] The amount of the actuarial adjustment changes on a sliding scale that increases each month that the individual delays claiming after the earliest date of eligibility.[107] Generally, the result is that a claimant receives a reduced amount of the PIA when claiming between age 62 and the individual's full retirement age, receives the full PIA when claiming at full retirement age, and receives an increased amount from the PIA if he claims any time between full retirement age and 70.[108] These actuarial adjustments are incredibly important because they are levied against the individual's benefit from the time of claiming until death. Once made, they are practically irreversible.[109]

In addition to affecting the amount that the individual receives, the actuarial adjustments can directly impact the amount that the spouse of the Social Security recipient will receive.[110] **The spouse of an individual who claims Social Security benefits is eligible to**

---

104 42 U.S.C. §§ 416(l), 402.

105 Ibid., § 402(a).

106 Ibid., § 402(q), (w); Social Security Handbook, § 720, 723.

107 Sidor, "Fact Sheet," 2–4. The exact amount of the actuarial adjustment varies within that range depending on the claimant's date of birth. Ibid.

108 42 U.S.C. § 402(q), (w); Social Security Handbook, §§ 720.3, 724.1. If the individual is working between FRA and 70, the benefit might be further increased because it could increase the PIA. Retirement Benefits, 7. For example, the PIA would increase if prior to 70, the individual worked for less than 35 years. Social Security Handbook, § 722.2.

109 20 C.F.R. § 404.640(b)(4) (2012); Sidor, "Fact Sheet," 2. The principle exception to this rule is that once made the individual can withdraw the application within 12 months. § 404.640(b)(4). However, the individual must pay back all benefits received from Social Security to date in one lump sum payment. Ibid. There is a large tax disadvantage to doing this because income tax paid by the individual on benefits received is not taken into consideration in the amount of repayment.

110 42 U.S.C. § 402(b), (e).

receive either a spousal benefit or a survivor benefit.[111] A spousal benefit can be claimed only when the Social Security recipient is still living, and the survivor benefit can be claimed only when the Social Security recipient is deceased.[112] The maximum that can be claimed as a spousal benefit is one half of the recipient's PIA, and the maximum that can be claimed as a survivor benefit is the decedent's entire PIA.[113] The PIA in this calculation must take into account any actuarial reductions incurred by the original claimant. [114]Additionally, actuarial reductions must also be calculated for the spouse who is claiming the spousal or survivor benefit based on the individual's age relative to the FRA at the time when the benefit is claimed.[115]

MAXIMIZING SOCIAL SECURITY BENEFITS FOR COUPLES: THE FILE AND SUSPEND STRATEGY

It is clear from the above that delaying claiming Social Security is beneficial to increasing lifetime income. The question for a couple considering when to claim then becomes, should we both just delay until age 70? The answer is no. **There are strategies that can be used to maximize Social Security benefits for couples that don't require both spouses to delay until they are 70 while receiving no benefit.** The principal strategy available to couples is the "File and Suspend" strategy.

---

111 Ibid., § 402(b), (e); Social Security Handbook, § 119.1.
112 42 U.S.C. § 402(b)(2), (e)(2)(A).
113 Ibid.
114 Ibid., § 402(q); Retirement Benefits, 9–10. The spousal or survivor benefit has reached it maximum when both spouses have reached FRA. § 402(q); Retirement Benefits, 9–10. Actuarial adjustments for spousal and survivor benefits can only reduce and never increase the benefit that the spouse receives. § 402(q); Retirement Benefits, 9–10.
115 Ibid., § 402(q)(3)(B)–(C).

The way that it works is that the youngest spouse would file and immediately suspend their benefit when they reach FRA. The older spouse is then permitted to claim a spousal-only benefit based off of the youngest spouse's PIA. Since there is no benefit to delaying claiming a spousal benefit after reaching FRA, the spousal benefit has been maximized. Meanwhile, the Social Security benefit of both spouses is continuing to increase. At age 70 the older spouse would then claim his or her benefit, which would be at its highest level. The younger spouse may in turn file for a spousal benefit based off of the older spouse's benefit. Finally, when the younger spouse reaches 70, he or she would then claim a Social Security benefit based on his or her own record. By doing this, both spouses have maximized their benefit from Social Security while receiving a benefit from Social Security during the interim.

Figure 4–B below shows an example of the assets and PIAs of a typical couple claiming Social Security. Figure 4–C shows the effect on the couple's retirement savings if they claim their benefit as soon as possible versus claiming using the File and Suspend strategy. This model assumes that the retirement spending of the retirees remains constant throughout retirement.

Figure 4–B: Client Example

Personal Information	John	Linda
Current Age	62	60
Claim Age Under F&S	68*	66
Claim ASAP Age	62	62

*John will then claim his own higher benefit at age 70

Social Security Benefits Information	Monthly	Annually
John's PIA at FRA	$1800	$21,600
Linda's PIA at FRA	$650	$7,800

John & Linda's Assets		
Non-Qualified Retirement Assets	$100,000	
Qualified Retirement Assets	John's IRA	Linda's IRA
Amount in Qualified Plan	$500,000	$150,000
Total Current Amount of Retirement Savings	$750,000	

Figure 4–C

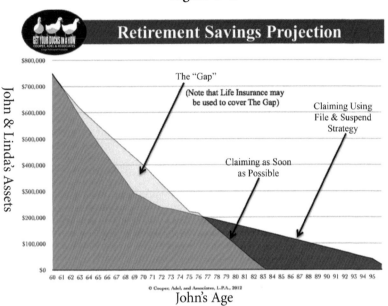

As shown in Figure 4–C, for this couple using the File and Suspend strategy allows the couple to continue their desired income for **11 years longer** than if they had claimed as soon as possible.

However, it also shows a fundamental concept that one must keep in mind when considering whether or not to use this strategy—the Gap. Figure 4–C shows that initially if the couple claims as soon as possible, they initially use more retirement assets to live because the couple is deferring current income to receive substantially higher income later in life. The benefit of the deferral is that when they later claim their benefits, they are significantly more than if they had claimed at the earliest possible age. This leads to an initial asset reduction for the couple that claims later. However, as you can see in Figure 4–C, the couple who claims later will eventually have more assets to sustain themselves during retirement because of the increased income. **We refer to this initial drop in assets as "the Gap."**

If both spouses both were to die during the Gap, then using this strategy leaves them with fewer assets than had they claimed as soon as possible. The Gap is critical because, if the couple does not account for it, they are essentially gambling their assets on the fact that they will live long enough to get past the Gap. However, there are ways to reduce this risk and bridge the Gap. One way to reduce the risk is that the couple gets a term life insurance policy during the Gap. By insuring themselves through the Gap, if one or both of them die, they get a fixed lump sum, which compensates them for the money they spent during the period of delaying claiming benefits. Therefore, this "bridge strategy" is a way you can have your cake and eat it too in order to maximize income and assets without risking your savings.

As the above example shows, longevity planning can be very beneficial but will normally require professional assistance. You need an advisor that will integrate the legal and financial elements.

OUR VIEW: Although the Social Security Trustees estimated in their 2013 Annual Report that the trust fund will be exhausted by 2033, it is not advisable to center your planning around the possibility that Social Security will no longer be around. We have seen many clients who are concerned about Social Security's solvency ask us if the best thing for them to do is to get as much as they can before it is no longer available. Their idea is that if they claim at the earliest possible age, even though they are taking the highest penalty, they would at least be getting something out of Social Security before it is no longer able to provide benefits anymore. However, we believe that this is not advisable.

If Social Security is reformed, we expect that the reforms will center around changes to claiming benefits and not simply a complete abatement of benefits. In our opinion, changes that could likely be made include: increasing the minimum retirement age, making penalties for claiming earlier than full-retirement age more significant, or offering more benefits for those who delay as long as possible. We think these are the most likely reforms because this is what Social Security has done in the past when they have faced similar solvency issues. For this reason we would never recommend claiming as early as possible simply out of concerns over Social Security's solvency. It highly unlikely that any future reform to Social Security would make it worth receiving a drastically reduced benefit for life.

OPTIMIZING INCOME FOR PRIVATE-SECTOR EMPLOYEES

Making sacrifices of assets in order to get more income for life is usually worth it. That being said, before considering whether and how to implement a strategy such as the File and Suspend strategy, it is important to note that optimizing income under longevity planning is not merely the maximization of income. Social Security claiming strategies should not be viewed in isolation. In longevity planning, the decision of when to claim Social Security benefits should be viewed in the context of existing assets and income tax planning. A retiree should ask two questions when considering using a strategy such as File and Suspend.

First, do I have enough assets to sustain myself through the Gap? If delaying claiming Social Security benefits would deplete the vast majority of assets by the end of the Gap, then delaying benefits may not be the best strategy. If that is your situation, your best decision may in fact be to claim as soon as possible. Or, if possible, you may consider working until 70, so you can still afford to delay claiming benefits without depleting your assets completely.

Second, what assets should I spend during the Gap? In order to optimize the benefit that will be received, the assets spent to supplement lower income during the Gap is very important. If available, the best assets to bridge the Gap are tax-deferred retirement assets, such as an IRA. This may seem like an uncomfortable idea, since most retirees consider their IRA their war chest. However, in the context of Social Security planning, you may discover that this "war chest" is in fact a Trojan Horse disguising a toxic asset. The reason is that if Social Security benefits are delayed as long as possible, to age 70, then 6 months later at 70½ the IRS mandates that you withdraw a certain amount annually from your IRA as a Required Minimum Distribution (RMD). So, at the time when the retiree is receiving social security benefits, they are also required to take RMDs from their IRA whether or not the retiree needs them. This could cause your income tax bracket to rise, putting you into a tax bracket where up to 85% of your Social Security benefits are taxable on top of the taxable income from the IRA. So, delaying benefits to maximize Social Security is not truly maximizing it if much of the benefit is lost to income tax.

The best strategy is to use money from tax-deferred accounts, such as IRAs, to support yourself during the Gap. Obviously, any money drawn out of the IRA would be taxable, but because during the Gap you would be older than 59½, you are not subject to any penalties for withdrawing it. During the Gap, the retiree does not have earned income or income from Social Security, so it is truly the perfect time to pay tax on your IRA. This will reduce the income tax impact of the RMDs on the future Social Security benefit and thereby maximize your Social Security benefits, providing for your future longevity.

OUR VIEW: Most longevity strategies are too risky for most people to try to plan on their own. Any sound longevity plan should be done with professional counsel. The plan should include both legal *and* financial planning since the principal risk in delaying Social Security is that something will happen to one or both of the recipients during the Gap. If individuals do not use a professional advisor to help them implement these strategies, they are not planning—they are gambling with their retirements.

PART III:
LONGEVITY PLANNING STRATEGIES FOR PUBLIC-SECTOR EMPLOYEES

INTRODUCTION TO THE GOVERNMENT PENSION OFFSET

The Government Pension Offset (GPO) adds another layer of complexity to the calculation of Social Security benefits. **It arises when the claimant is a government worker and is married to, or the widow of, an individual who is eligible for Social Security.** [116]There are five exceptions to the GPO, none of which would apply to the average state, city, or municipal government employee who has recently retired or will be retiring in the future.[117] Other

---

116 20 C.F.R. § 404.408a (2012).

117 Ibid., § 404.408a(b). The five exemptions occur when the government employee: (1) has a government pension based on employment for an interstate instrumentality, (2) received or was eligible to receive a government pension for one or more months in the period of December 1977 through November 1982, (3) was receiving or was eligible to receive a government pension for one or more months before July 1983, (4) would have been eligible for a pension during one of the aforementioned months except for a requirement which delayed eligibility for such pension until the month following the month in which all other requirements were met, or (5) is receiving a government pension based wholly upon service as a member of a uniformed service. Ibid.

than these exceptions, which are largely inapplicable, there are no other restrictions to the application of the GPO.[118] There is no minimum amount that triggers the application of the offset, so it applies to all public pensions, large or small.[119] Additionally, the offset is calculated using the individual's assessed monthly public pension amount, even if a lump-sum distribution is utilized and the amount that is actually received is greatly reduced by penalties or taxes.[120]

The calculation of the offset is different for the spousal as opposed to the survivor benefit. For the spousal benefit, the GPO subtracts two-thirds of the monthly government pension benefit from half of the spouse's PIA (less any actuarial reductions that the spouse incurred).[121] For the survivor benefit, the GPO subtracts two-thirds of the monthly government pension benefit from the spouse's entire PIA (less any actuarial reductions that the spouse incurred).[122] If the number is less than zero, then under the GPO the claimant receives no benefit.[123] If greater than zero, the claimant receives the result of that calculation as a monthly benefit from Social Security.[124]

To demonstrate, consider the claiming decisions of one Ohio couple, Larry and Linda. Larry worked at a job where he

---

118 See Ibid., § 404.408a. There is however one exception whereby an individual is be exempted from the GPO by being employed in a job for 60 months where the individual contributed to Social Security. See Social Security Protection Act of 2004, Pub. L. No. 108-203, (codified as amended at 42 U.S.C. § 402(k) (2004)). pp. 31–33.

119 See 20 C.F.R. § 404.408a.

120 Ibid., § 404.408a(a). Were this regulation not in place, the individual would be treated as though he/she has no government pension, if the government pension benefit was withdrawn as a lump sum. This would result in the individual receiving both the lump sum distribution from the public pension and a full spousal or survivor benefit from Social Security.

121 42 U.S.C. § 402(b)(2) (2006); Ibid., § 404.408a(a), (d)(1)–(2).

122 42 U.S.C. § 402(e)(2)(A); 20 C.F.R. § 404.408a(d)(1)–(2).

123 20 C.F.R. § 404.408a(d)(1)–(2).

124 Ibid.

contributed to Social Security with a resulting PIA of $2,000. Linda, Larry's spouse, is due a monthly pension of $1,125 from the State Teacher's Retirement System (STRS). Figure 4–D, summarizes the difference in the monthly benefit amount based on when benefits are claimed.

Figure 4–D: Larry and Linda's Potential Claiming Benefits

Claiming Social Security & the GPO	Larry's SS Benefit	Linda's Public Pension Benefit		
	SS Benefit	Public Pension Benefit	SS Spousal Benefit	SS Survivor Benefit
Claiming ASAP (at age 62)	$1,650	$1,125	$0	$900
Claiming at FRA	$2,000	$1,125	$250	$1,250
Claiming at 70	$2,640	$1,125	$250	$1,250

As the above figure shows, if Larry claims the benefit at the earliest time possible, he will receive an actuarial reduction of 82.5%, and the resulting monthly benefit will be $1,650. If Linda attempts to claim a spousal benefit as early as possible, then the benefit amount that would be offset would again be decreased by 82.5%, and the maximum potential benefit would be around $680. Lastly, because Linda has a public pension benefit, the $680 would further be subject to the GPO. The amount of the offset would be $750, and since that exceeds the potential spousal benefit, Linda would not receive any spousal benefit from Social Security.[125]

Conversely, had Larry waited until his FRA to claim the benefit, he would receive a monthly benefit not subject to actuarial reductions and equal to his PIA of $2,000. If Linda waits until her FRA to claim a spousal benefit, then she would not be subject to any actuarial reductions, and the maximum benefit she could receive

---

125 The amount of the offset, $750, was found by taking two-thirds of the public pension benefit of $1,125.

is $1,000. This benefit would still be subject to the GPO, which imposes an offset of $750. However, because both of them delayed claiming benefits until their FRAs, Linda would receive a monthly spousal benefit of $250 from Social Security.

This difference, caused by delaying claiming until FRA, is especially important if the public pension benefit is ever reduced. As the above example shows, the difference, caused by delaying claiming until FRA, could make the difference between receiving and not receiving a benefit from Social Security. This disparity becomes even larger if the public pension benefit is ever reduced, because the ongoing benefit after the reduction will be greater. This is because, as shown in the previous example, the number that is being offset against (the $750 versus $1000) is larger.

In summary, an individual whose spousal or survivor benefit from Social Security is subject to the GPO, will either receive no benefit or a substantially reduced benefit. Given that the survivor benefit is computed using the entire PIA and a spousal benefit is computed using only half of the PIA, it is common that a government employee is eligible for a survivor benefit but not a spousal benefit.

How and When Should We Claim? A Case Study of Longevity Planning in Ohio

Taking into account and planning based off of the specific features of an individual's public pension system is vital to constructing a proper longevity plan for public-sector employees. It would be impossible to explain all of the intricacies of every state, city, and municipal pension system. That being said, there are some common features present in almost all state, city, and municipal pension plans. Most offer the employee the option to make an election that would provide a monthly survivor benefit payable after the retiree's death, but taking this election reduces the amount that the employee receives during retirement. In addition, most offer a way for a government employee to take a lump sum distribution in lieu of a monthly pension, but impose significant penalties on such distributions.

The State Teacher's Retirement System of Ohio (STRS Ohio) has both of these features and also a few unique options that should serve as a good example of the intricacies that could be present in other systems. Another similarity between STRS Ohio and other public pension benefit systems around the country is that the Ohio legislature recently passed pension reform. **These two aspects make STRS Ohio a good case study to demonstrate the complex decisions that must be made in constructing a longevity plan for current government retirees** as they attempt to determine how and when it is the most beneficial for them to claim both their public pension benefit as well as their spousal or survivor benefit in light of the GPO.

Ohio is a state that manages its own public pension benefit system. [126]One of the systems that the state of Ohio has put into place is STRS Ohio, which serves approximately 476,000 of Ohio's retired and active educators and purports to be one of the "nation's premier retirement systems."[127] That being said, on September 12, 2012, Ohio's General Assembly instituted pension reforms that affected the amount of pension benefits that will be received by both current and future retirees.[128] The most significant difference

---

126 Federal State Reference Guide, IRS, Pub. 963, http://www.irs.gov/pub/irs-pdf/p963.pdf, 1-1 ¬to 1-2.
127 "About STRS Ohio," State Teachers Retirement System of Ohio, https://www.strsoh. org/about/index.html, Mar 11, 2013; see generally "Ohio Revised Code Annotated" § 3307 (West 2012).
128 Ibid.

imposed is a change in the Cost of Living Adjustment (COLA) given to current and future retirees. For current retirees, there will be no COLA increase in the year 2014, but in 2015 the COLA will be reinstituted at a fixed rate of 2%.[129] Future retirees who retire after July 2013 will have to wait five years before receiving their first COLA increase.[130]

COLAs are designed to keep the benefit amount substantially level throughout the years despite inflation. In any given year, if inflation exceeds the COLA, then the recipient has actually received a reduction in benefits. Therefore, depending on inflation, the changes made to the COLA through the Ohio pension reforms could result in a significant reduction for future retirees. In light of these potential reductions, the issues that longevity planning should incorporate for future retirees under STRS Ohio is twofold: first, *how* they should claim their public pension benefit; and second, *when* they should claim their spousal and survivor benefits.

The first part of the claiming decision is *how* to claim the public pension benefits. Under STRS Ohio, the individual retiree has two choices: (1) whether or not to accept a reduced pension benefit in order to receive a spousal or survivor benefit, and (2) whether to take a full lump sum distribution, a partial lump sum distribution, or elect a full pension benefit with no lump sum distribution. [131]Presumably, if the benefits would ever be reduced drastically in the future, it would be best to maximize the benefit that is received from the outset by electing the full lump sum option. Additionally, it is important to keep in mind that in many of the pension reforms that have been enacted, the spousal and

129 Ibid.; "Ohio Approves Pension Reform," State Teachers Retirement System of Ohio, Oct 2012, https://www.strsoh.org/pdfs/44-920G.pdf, 1–2.

130 Ohio S.B. 342; "Ohio Approves Pension Reform," 1–2.

131 STRS Ohio has what is known as a Partial Lump Sum Option Plan (PLOP), which is an example of the intricacies that are available in some public pension plans but not in others. See "PLOP Information," State Teachers Retirement System of Ohio, https://www.strsoh.org/active/2e01.html, Mar 11, 2013.

survivor benefits have been reduced.[132] So, if you decide to forego some of your benefits in order to provide an income for your spouse in the future, you could instead end up receiving less now, and because of pension reform, less in the future. This would lead to the conclusion that it would be best to take no spousal benefit and to consider taking a partial or full lump sum distribution. On the other hand, if the individual receives an unreduced pension benefit for a long period, then it would be inadvisable to take a partial or lump sum distribution of the pension benefits because of the penalties imposed by STRS Ohio and the potential income tax consequences.

The second part of the claiming decision is *when* to claim the public pension benefit and when to claim a spousal and survivor benefit from Social Security. When the individual claims the benefit, it will be subject to the GPO, regardless of how they choose to claim the public pension benefit. If you choose a lump sum distribution option, the GPO is still calculated using the gross monthly benefit amount without taking into account either income taxes or the penalties imposed by STRS. As such, the decisions with the biggest impact to the spousal or survivor Social Security benefit is when the benefit is claimed by the Social Security recipient and when the benefit is claimed by the spouse.

Further, if your public pension benefit is reduced either by pension reform or bankruptcy, then the amount of the Social Security benefit will be incredibly important to maintaining your lifestyle throughout retirement. In order to be less dependent on a government pension benefit that could later be reduced, it would seem that the claimants would want to avoid actuarial reductions in benefits in order maximize what they could receive from Social Security. This strategy is not applicable to all situations. For example, if the life expectancy of either spouse is very low due to a critical illness, or if they do not make enough money to make it through the period while they are delaying claiming benefits, this strategy would not be advisable. If the person who delayed claiming benefits passes away before or soon after claiming the benefit, then that individual has had several years where they have claimed no benefit and not enough years where the increased benefit has been received. However, for a couple of normal life expectancy, if both spouses delay until their FRA, they will be more insulated in the event that the public pension benefit is ever reduced. The level of uncertainty and amount of client-specific planning that these decisions require makes it imperative that you seek legal advice in making these claiming decisions. Further, the advice that you seek must take into account these decisions in the context of an overall longevity plan.

SUMMARY

Whether you are a private- or public-sector employee, it is essential that you incorporate longevity planning into your existing healthcare and estate planning. If you do not take longevity planning into account, you could plan your retirement over an inaccurately short of a period of time. This could lead to making improper planning decisions that could lead you to outlive your assets. Since under Obamacare, seniors will be responsible for paying for more for their care, this lack of assets could lead you to a lack of availability of care. The use of longevity planning could make you more able to afford the care you need and also give you the ability to seek alternative options for care.

The most important component to longevity planning is the optimization of income, and the biggest sources of income for most baby boomers will be Social Security and public pension benefits. As such, making strategic decisions in claiming these benefits is possibly the most consequential decision a baby boomer will make in planning for retirement. Baby boomers should seek planning that incorporates appropriate legal and financial products and takes into account all of the assets. Seeking the proper advice is critical because once the claiming decisions are made, they are almost always permanent and irreversible, as are their consequences upon retirees. In short, longevity planning can make the difference between a happy, comfortable retirement and one of shortages and heartache.

> **OUR VIEW**: We believe that, even though Social Security does have some funding problems, it is a much more stable system than public pension systems. The public pension systems serve a small sector of retirees in comparison to the segment of the population that is reliant on Social Security. Therefore, Social Security is more likely than public pension systems to receive assistance in sustaining itself. This is evidenced by the fact that many public pension systems have already been allowed to declare bankruptcy or implement drastic reforms without any sort of bailout or government assistance. For this reason we advise that couples in which one spouse receives Social Security and the other receives a government pension, should plan to maximize their Social Security, even if it is at the expense of receiving less of a public pension benefit.

THE TAKEAWAY:
THE WHY AND HOW OF LONGEVITY PLANNING

- The proper measure of life expectancy is measured from retirement, not birth. Current life expectancy from retirement is 84 for men and 86 for women, which is 7 years longer than life expectancy estimates from birth.

- Underestimating longevity could lead to a fundamentally flawed retirement plan that only provides for a fraction of your retirement needs.

- The cornerstone of longevity planning is planning for income, but such planning should be to optimize income—not merely maximize it.

- There are vital claiming decisions that will be faced by all private- and public-sector employees, and using the proper or improper strategy will have drastic and irreversible effects on the retirees' incomes for the rest of their lives.

- Private-sector employees should consider using a coordinated strategy, such as the File and Suspend strategy, to delay claiming benefits.

- Public-sector employees should carefully plan the elections that they make when claiming their pension, such as electing to have a spousal benefit. Also, they must keep in mind how they will be affected by provisions such as the Government Pension Offset.

- This area is so complex that professional assistance is a necessity.

- Longevity planning is necessary to insulate yourself from, and give yourself options despite, the increased healthcare costs for seniors that are expected to follow the implementation of Obamacare.

SECTION 2:
HOW WILL I ACCESS CARE?

"As baby boomers, we never had enough seats in the classroom, never enough teachers, never enough jobs, never enough of anything. Now, we will face a crisis in healthcare. There will simply not be enough dollars to allow us all access to the care we need. We need options."

—Rick Law, Elder Law Attorney

Chicago, Illinois

Chapter 5:

Learning From the Mistakes of Others—Larger Demand, Lower Supply, and Longer Waits

Facing Obamacare in our own backyard, what can we learn from other countries with long-standing government-run healthcare systems? Consider that Canada, a country ranked the per capita most highly educated country in the world, does not have an adequate supply of doctors to provide quality care to their small population, which is only about three times the size of Ohio.[133] Looking to the United Kingdom, a country with one of the largest GDPs in the world and a drive to contain healthcare costs, we find that they also face a doctor shortage, and they have patients who wait weeks and months for critical medical procedures. Ironically, even though an elderly queen sits at the head of the monarchy, problems in the U.K.'s healthcare system affect the elderly more than any other group.

It follows that we will experience similar issues as the new healthcare laws take effect in the U.S. over the next few years. Interestingly, we have already had some experience here at home with Massachusetts, where a massive healthcare reform act became law in 2006. To understand what we may be facing in the coming years, we will examine the impact of universal healthcare

---

133 Feb 3, 2012, "Canada Tops List of the Most Educated Countries," NBC News, http://www.nbcnews.com/business/canada-tops-list-most-educated-countries-1C7100865

in Canada, then in England, and finally, within our own borders, in Massachusetts.

PART I: CANADA—SHORT ON DOCTORS, LONG ON WAIT TIME

The common denominator between the current healthcare system in Canada and the future reformed healthcare system in the U.S. is likely to be an inadequate supply of doctors to meet the increasing demand of formerly uninsured patients. We can look to Canada, where universal care in various forms has been in place since first enacted in 1968, as a harbinger of things to come in our country. In this section we will review the basis on which Canada built its healthcare plan, the similarities and differences with Obamacare, and the factors that led to the doctor shortage in Canada, as well as the impact of having fewer doctors.

CANADA AND THE U.S.: WHAT ARE WE MISSING?

Both Canada and the U.S. (beginning in 2014) require citizens to participate in health insurance plans. Canada's Health Act leaves governance of healthcare insurance plans to individual provinces that provide services through private entities but mandate common features and basic standards of coverage.[134] In much the same way, Obamacare will offer both state-operated and federally-funded exchanges through which residents can access private healthcare insurance plans, and, like Canada, will require

---

134 "Canada Health Act—Frequently Asked Questions," Health Canada, http://www.hc-sc.gc.ca/hcs-sss/medi-assur/faq-eng.php

common features and basic standards of coverage. Private clinics are available in Canada but are subject to predetermined fees set by the government. Health insurance is also available, but it is used as "supplements" for services not covered or only partially covered by Canada's medical care. For example, the private-sector plans cover prescription drugs, dentistry, optometry, and plastic surgery.[135] Canada has no lifetime limits or pre-existing condition exclusions and does not withhold services based on employment status, income, or health status. Other than the care for those over 65, this is similar to the upcoming plan for the U.S.

Canada's provinces are "responsible for their own healthcare including financing, planning, and evaluating the provisions of hospital care, negotiating salaries of health professionals and negotiating fees for physician services."[136] However, the federal government has the mandate to ensure quality of care through federal standards. A big difference between Canada and the U.S. is that Canadian patients may not be charged for insured services, and they are not involved in billing or reimbursement for services. Further, there is no variety in Canadian healthcare plans as "all essential basic care has been covered" and their co-pays are very low or nonexistent in most provinces.[137] Canadian doctors are compensated by the government with a mix of fee-for-service and salary compensation.[138]

---

135 "Everything you ever wanted to know about Canadian health care in one post," Washington Post, http://www.washingtonpost.com/blogs/wonkblog/wp/2012/07/01/everything-you-ever-wanted-to-know-about-canadian-health-care-in-one-post/
136 Benedict Irvine, "Background Briefing: The Canadian Health Care System," http://www.civitas.org.uk/pdf/Canada.pdf
137 "An Overview of the Canadian Health Care System," http://assets.ce.columbia.edu/pdf/actu/actu-canada.pdf
138 http://ce.columbia.edu/files/ce/pdf/actu/actu-canada.pdf

IN THE FACE OF A SHORTAGE, CUTS IN MEDICAL STUDENTS AND RESIDENTS

Figure 5-A: The Location and Professional Activity of Canadian Medical School Graduates

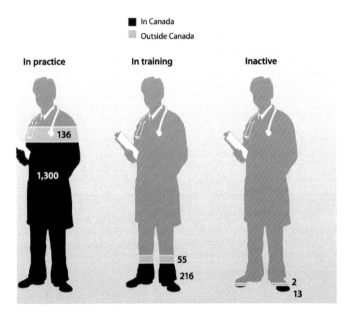

Canada's shortage of doctors began when medical school enrollment was cut in response to a study in the early 1990s that predicted a surplus of physicians.[139] The Canadian government acted on the recommendations of the Barer-Stoddart study by cutting the number of medical students, residents, and positions available for foreign doctors. Canada has fewer than 70,000 physicians and surgeons for its population of over 34 million, or about 2 physicians per 1,000 people.[140] In contrast, member

---

139 "Canada's Physician Supply," Fraser Forum, March/April 2011, http://www.fraserinstitute.org/uploadedFiles/fraser-ca/Content/research-news/research/articles/canadas-physician-supply.pdf

140 "Health Crisis—Canada Needs Thousands of Doctors Now (2011)," BC Chamber of Commerce, http://www.bcchamber.org/advocacy/policy/provincial_gov/health/canada_needs_thousands_of_doctors_now.html

countries of the OECD, the Organization for Economic Co-operation and Development (34 countries, including the U.S. and most developed countries), have an average of 2.7 physicians per 1,000 people. From these numbers we can conclude that Canada needs an estimated 20,000 (+29%) new physicians immediately.

Even though Canada has increased the number of positions available, they are still far behind demand, due to the planning and cost-cutting efforts in the 1990s to avoid a doctor surplus. Thus, as shown in Figure 5–A, there are not enough spots for everyone in Canadian Medical Schools. Rationing-related studies cut their place in the line.

REGULATIONS PREVENT FOREIGN DOCTORS FROM FILLING THE GAP

One solution offered to alleviate the shortage of doctors in Canada is to attract physicians and surgeons from other countries, so-called International Medical Graduates (IMGs). Approximately 25% of all physicians and surgeons in Canada are IMGs. However, due to Canadian government regulations, IMGs are required to complete residency in Canada to meet the requirements of the medical colleges who regulate medical practice licensing. There are currently 1,200 IMGs in Canada waiting to obtain their license. [141]Why are they "waiting"? At the core of the problem is once again a shortage of residency and post-graduate positions that are regulated and rationed by the provinces. Cost containment has cut their place in the line.

If only 1,200 IMGs are in the queue for residency positions, and they need 20,000+, how will Canada meet the medical needs of

141 Ibid.

their country? Some Canadians have taken an alternate approach. **In fact, over 46,000 Canadians sought medical care in another country in 2011, an increase of 104% from 1993, rather than waiting in line for services that may never be available to them.**[142]

A Dearth of Doctors Leaves Orphaned Patients

The greatest doctor shortage in Canada is among family and primary care doctors. According to the Canadian Medical Association, an estimated 4 to 5 million (11%) Canadians are so-called "orphan patients" who have no family physician. Even doctors themselves are not immune from the problem. Over 70% of Canada's physicians and surgeons have no doctor for their own care.[143] Once again, cost containment appears to have cut their place in the line.

Physicians and surgeons who are in practice in Canada also struggle to meet the demand of their patients as cost containment has imposed stringent work-hour restrictions. Cost containment has created clusters of patients waiting to see their doctors. As shown below in Figure 5–B and Figure 5–C, in 2011, **the average Canadian in need of medical care could expect to wait 19 weeks from the required general practitioner (GP) referral to treatment by a specialist in Canada.**[144] Half of that wait time was to see the specialist for a consultation and the other half was wait time before treatment began.

142 Nadeem Esmail, "Leaving Canada for medical care," Fraser Forum, July/August 2012, http://www.fraserinstitute.org/uploadedFiles/fraser-ca/Content/research-news/research/articles/leaving-canada-for-medical-care-2011-ff0712.pdf
143 "Health Crisis—Canada Needs Thousands of Doctors Now (2011)."
144 Bacchus Barua, Mark Rovere, and Brett J. Skinner, "Waiting Your Turn: Wait Times for Health Care in Canada 2011 Report," Studies in Health Policy, (Fraser Institute, December 2011), http://www.fraserinstitute.org/uploadedFiles/fraser-ca/Content/research-news/research/publications/waiting-your-turn-2011.pdf

Figure 5-B: Median Wait by Province in 2011 Weeks Waited from Referral by GP to Treatments

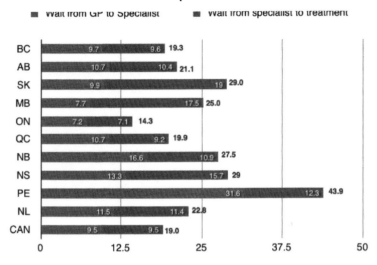

■ Wait from GP to Specialist   ■ Wait from specialist to treatment

As you see in Figure 5–B, the median wait to see a GP and a specialist varies depending where you live. The supply, demand, and facilities are different in every province. In addition to the long wait for an appointment, there were also long delays for diagnostic services and surgery, as shown in Figure 5–C:

■ Wait from GP to Specialist   ■ Wait from specialist to treatment

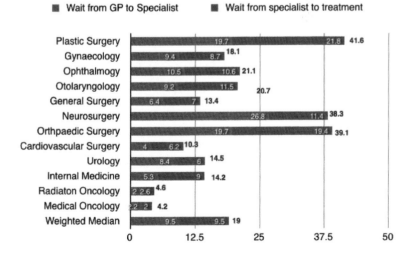

- 4 weeks for a CT scan

- 4.6 weeks for an ultrasound scan

- 9.2 weeks for an MRI scan

- 21 weeks for eye, ear, nose, or throat surgery

- 38 weeks for neurosurgery

- 39 weeks for orthopedic surgery (e.g. knees, hips)[145]

Testimonial

Sharon McGuin, an elderly patient from Windsor, Ontario, visited her family doctor. Her doctor referred her to an orthopedic surgeon to get a knee replacement. Unfortunately, she had a year-and-a-half wait to see the orthopedic surgeon. She grew frustrated of the pain and the strong pain medication. She finally decided to go abroad like thousands of Canadians do every year, even though care outside Canada is not free. The pain was too much.[146]

HOW DOES THIS COMPARE TO HISTORICAL WAITING PERIODS IN THE U.S.?

In an article in the journal *Health Affairs*, Robert Blendon describes an international survey of hospital administrators in Australia, New Zealand, Great Britain, the U.S., and Canada. "When asked for the average waiting time for biopsy of a possible breast cancer in a 50-year-old woman, 21 percent of administrators of Canadian

---

145 Ibid
146 "Canadian Medical Tourism," http://www.youtube.com/watch?v=pWKiFf8qAWE

hospitals said more than three weeks; only 1 percent of American hospital administrators gave the same answer." In the same survey, "Fifty percent of the Canadian hospital administrators said the average waiting time for a 65-year-old man who requires a routine hip replacement was more than six months; in contrast, not one American hospital administrator reported waiting periods that long. For example, 86% of American hospital administrators said the average waiting time was shorter than three weeks; only 3% of Canadian hospital administrators said their patients have this brief a wait. Figure 5–D shows the percentage of different countries' patients that waited four weeks or more to see a specialist.

Figure 5-D: Waiting Time of Four Weeks or More for a Specialist Appointment

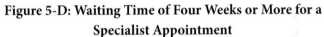

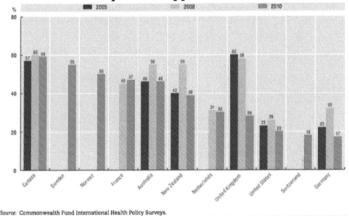

Source: Commonwealth Fund International Health Policy Surveys.

StatLink ㎑ http://dx.doi.org/10.1787/888932526008

In 2011, the wait time for treatment after an appointment with a specialist was 42% longer than what Canadian physicians consider to be clinically reasonable, according to a national survey of physicians.[147] Studies examining the adverse consequences of long wait times have found:

---

147 Barua et al. "Waiting Your Turn."

- An increased likelihood of hospitalization and emergency admissions

- Poorer outcomes following treatment

- Increased likelihood of death

Canadian cost-cutting strategies have also affected their ability to keep up with current technology that should be available to their patients. For example, "an estimated 60% of their radiological equipment is technically outdated."[148]

The cost of cuts in Canada's universal healthcare system have led to severe setbacks for both patients and doctors. When patients feel they are not getting proper care, they will seek care elsewhere even if it comes at a greater financial cost to them. A study performed by a research team at Simon Fraser University in British Columbia, Canada, found that "30 of the 32 interviewees [94% of those who had traveled abroad for care] indicated that they would go abroad for care again should the need arise." The majority of patients traveling abroad to access care did so because of "waiting times domestically, increased treatment options abroad, lower costs for care abroad, and the high quality of care available abroad."[149]

Testimonials

Terry Salo from BC, Canada, needed his left hip replaced urgently. He was suffering from depression as the pain of his every movement was becoming more difficult to overcome. Instead of waiting for months or years to

---

148 "High-Priced Pain: What to Expect from a Single-Payer Health Care System," The Heritage Foundation, http://www.heritage.org/research/reports/2006/09/high-priced-pain-what-to-expect-from-a-single-payer-health-care-system
149 Crooks, Valoris, et al., Perspectives on Canadians' Involvement in Medical Tourism,

receive treatment in Canada, he flew to the front of the line by going to India for relief. He was so happy with the results and experience that two years later he went back to have his right hip replaced.[150]

Jeff Clark suffered from severe back pain for years. He visited three orthopedic doctors. Because of the overloaded Canadian healthcare system it took three years to see the required doctors. Even when he was able to get in to see these doctors, they had nothing to offer him. He decided to travel to Chennai, India, where diagnostic testing identified his problem as a severely damaged disk. His doctor, who was trained in England, explained to him what was wrong and how they were going to fix it.[151]

Part II:
U.K.—Cost Containment at the Expense of the Elderly

On the other side of the Atlantic, the United Kingdom has had universal healthcare in place since shortly after World War II, in response to broad consensus that healthcare should be available to all.[152] Since then, the program, under the direction of the National Health Service (NHS), has grown to be the world's largest publicly funded health service.[153] The original mission of the NIHS was to devise best practices for medicine.

150 CBC News, http://www.youtube.com/watch?v=ZrDilwBC9E8

151 "Medical testimonial," http://www.surgicaltourism.ca/

152 Donald W. Light, NCBI, "Universal Health Care: Lessons from the British Experience," http://www.ncbi.nlm.nih.gov/pmc/articles/PMC1447686/

153 http://www.nhs.uk/NHSEngland/thenhs/about/Pages/overview.aspx

The U.K. has a different paradigm for determining the care that you will receive as a patient than our current system here in the U.S. In the U.S. today, your doctor focuses on your individual symptoms to determine the course of treatment, tempered to some degree by your ability to pay privately, through benefits from Medicare or Medicaid, or through group or private health insurance. **In the U.K., a government-run board sets the standards for your doctor that determine your course of treatment based on whether the cost of care is more than the value of your life.**[154] Direct taxation, rather than insurance or private monies, funds the NHS.

The National Institute for Health and Clinical Excellence (NICE) was set up in the U.K. to "ensure that every treatment, operation, or medicine used is the proven best. It will root out under-performing doctors and useless treatments, spreading best practices everywhere." This underlying philosophy is very similar to that underlying our own Obamacare. **The difference is that time and experience have directed the focus of national policy away from treatment and toward overall cost containment.** Unfortunately, "Britain . . . ultimately has concluded that it can only rein in costs by limiting care."[155] In practice, NICE has reduced cost based on **WHO** you are and **WHERE** you live. NICE-imposed cost constraints further limit **WHAT** you can receive across the board.

UNIVERSAL CARE? WHO YOU ARE MAKES A DIFFERENCE

Universal healthcare in the U.K. has not improved the numerous elderly patients who are being denied medical treatment based

154 "QALYs and Policy Evaluation: A New Perspective," Yale Journal of Health Policy, Law and Ethics, http://digitalcommons.law.yale.edu/cgi/viewcontent.cgi?article=1128&context=yjhple
155 "Of NICE and Men," Wall Street Journal, http://online.wsj.com/article/SB124692973435303415.html

on standards set by NICE. NICE imposes a process whereby the quality-weighted years an individual might expect to add to their lives as a result of the proposed medical procedure, adjusted for their life expectancy, determines whether or not the expenditure is approved.[156] Although not a feature of the current Obamacare plan, the fact remains that there are three compelling forces converging in the near future that might force the U.S. to adopt a similar system: (1) the cuts in Medicare and Medicaid reimbursements to hospitals and insurers anticipated with Obamacare, (2) the sheer number of baby boomers who will flood the Medicare system at the same time the reimbursement is reduced, and (3) the reduced number of younger taxpayers who are available to foot the bill for Medicare. What is the likely outcome? Here is an example of how it works in the U.K.:

> Kenneth Warden is an elderly Brit who was diagnosed with terminal bladder cancer. "His hospital consultant sent him home to die, ruling that at 78 he was too old to treat. Even the palliative surgery or chemotherapy that could have eased his distressing symptoms was declared off-limits because of his age." [157]

> His distraught daughter, Michele Halligan, accepted the sad prognosis but looked for a second opinion. An out-of-pocket private doctor then took the case. "Thanks to her tenacity, Kenneth got the drugs and surgery he needed—and as a result his cancer was actually cured." [158]

---

156 "QALYs and Policy Evaluation."
157 "Sentenced to Death for being Old: The NHS Denies Life-Saving Treatment to Elderly, as one Man's Chilling Story Reveals," MailOnline.com, April 6, 2012, http://www.dailymail.co.uk/health/article-2126379/Sentenced-death-old-The-NHS-denies-life-saving-treatment-elderly-mans-chilling-story-reveals.html
158 Ibid.

Kenneth's story is predictive of what could and probably will happen to the elderly in America. "According to . . . the Macmillan Cancer Support, every year many thousands of older people are routinely denied life-saving National Health Service (NHS) treatments because their doctors write them off as too old to treat."[159]

In addition to what is operationally age discrimination, the U.K. recognizes other factors that penalize certain classes of its citizens. For instance, a North Staffordshire hospital "is tackling its £30 million (US$47 million) of NHS debt by restricting access to surgery among obese patients."[160] Knee and hip replacement services are being denied to patients with a body mass index measurement of 30. This reduced the hospital's joint replacement patients by an estimated 25%.[161]

As the U.S. faces obesity challenges in the future among all age groups, it is likely that policies such as those in the U.K. will become the only alternative for Uncle Sam to keep our skyrocketing healthcare costs, which were already growing at a faster rate than our GDP, in check. Kaiser Health reports that health spending will account for close to 20% of the GDP in 2021, up from nearly 18% in 2010.[162]

---

159 Ibid.
160 "MMS 2013 Public Opinion Survey Shows High Satisfaction With Health Care, Easy Access to Care, But Cost, Affordability Remain Most Important Issue," Massachusetts Medical Society, http://www.massmed.org/News-and-Publications/MMS-News-Releases/MMS-2013-Public-Opinion-Survey-Shows--High-Satisfaction-with-Health-Care,-Easy-Access-to-Care,--But-Cost,-Affordability-Remain-Most-Important-Issues/#.UgKy92Rgafs
161 Ibid.
162 "Report: Health Spending Will Clime to Nearly One-Fifth of GDP," Kaiser Health News, http://capsules.kaiserhealthnews.org/index.php/2012/06/report-health-spending-will-climb-to-nearly-one-fifth-of-gdp/

Universal Care? Where You Live Makes a Difference

One might assume that "universal" healthcare would mean that care would be the same for all, regardless of socioeconomic class or location. In the U.K., that has not been the case. One analysis of the NHS showed that *where* you were first treated for cancer predicted whether you would receive additional anti-cancer treatment after surgery. Survival rates ranged from 64% to 84% depending on the regional health board delivering the healthcare.[163] Further, residents of northern England, who are primarily the old and poor, are twice as likely to die of cancer than those from southern England.

One unintended consequence of centralizing service centers in urban areas has further reduced services to residents of more rural areas. As Gordon Baird, a spokesperson for the Royal College of General Practitioners, describes, "In my own area of rural Scotland, some cancer patients have to travel up to 14 hours in a single day to make out-patient appointments. This is wholly unacceptable and people's chances of recovery are being directly reduced as a result. Cancer patients need the appropriate level of care close to where they live."[164] We must consider that we are already facing a doctor shortage in the rural areas of the U.S. Will cost constraints or centralizing care in clinics cause further strain on the rural population?

---

163 "MPs attack cancer care 'lottery,'" BBC, January 2005, http://news.bbc.co.uk/2/hi/health/4203625.stm
164 Ibid.

Universal Care? Universal Cutbacks of WHAT is Available

To keep costs down, the number of beds in U.K. hospitals is kept under control. "Indeed, a shortage of intensive care unit (ICU) beds in the NHS has contributed to patient deaths. In 2000, the NHS had 9 critical care beds per 100,000, compared to 31 per 100,000 in the United States. In a review of deaths following surgery in the NHS, some 40% of hospitals with preoperative deaths had no ICU beds at all. In 61 cases (5% of those who died), the patients were denied access to ICU beds because no bed was available."[165]

In a further move to keep costs down, the U.K. standardizes reimbursement for surgeries, which has led to a reduction in the number of more complex procedures, such as orthopedic operations, which cannot be performed because the reimbursement does not match the cost. For example, a four-hour hip operation with eight follow-up days of inpatient physiotherapy costs £13,791 (US$21,562), but the reimbursement paid by the Department of Health was only £4,967 ($7,766). That is less than 36% of the real cost of the procedure.

> OUR VIEW: We believe that the United Kingdom serves as a harbinger of things to come here in the States. With almost 70 years of experience with universal healthcare, and a historical culture similar to our own, it is likely that we in this country are going to walk down the same path in our own healthcare system of "cost containment trumping treatment." Indeed the controversial Independent Patient Advisory Board (IPAB) contained as part of Obamacare

---

165 E. Bennett-Guerrero, J. A. Hyam S. Shaefi, D. R. Prytherch, G. L. Sutton, P. C. Weaver, M. G. Mythen, M. P. Grocott, and M. K. Parides, "Comparison of P-POSSUM Risk-Adjusted Mortality Rates After Surgery Between Patients in the U.S.A and the U.K.," British Journal of Surgery 90, No. 12 (December 2003), 1593–1598.

(discussed at length in Chapter 6) has as its goal to "reduce the per capita rate of growth in Medicare spending"[166] All of this is supposed to be done while maintaining the same quality of medical care. Only time will tell, but we can only hope that we do not end up, as has England, at a point where your course of treatment is based on whether the cost of care is more than the value of your life.[167] It is an old maxim that we should hope for the best, but plan for the worst. For this reason we believe that our clients must plan to privately pay for and travel for healthcare.

PART III:
MASSACHUSETTS—HIGHEST MARKET PREMIUMS IN THE COUNTRY

Closer to home, in 2006, then-governor Mitt Romney signed into law the Massachusetts Healthcare Reform Law, sometimes called "Romneycare," to provide state-regulated insurance coverage to every resident and free insurance to those earning less than 150% of the federal poverty level. However, this bill was not presented and passed entirely for humanitarian reasons. Romney observed that Massachusetts was spending "almost $1 billion on free care for the uninsured" prior to his bill. [168]

Provisions of Romneycare have often been compared to Obamacare, including provisions such as "insurance mandates, plus tough rules for when employers must offer plans and the

---

166 Sara Margolis, "Independent Payment Advisory Board Review Put on Hold," Columbia Business Law Review Online, http://cblr.columbia.edu/archives/11968
167 "QALYs and Policy Evaluation."
168 "Massachusetts' Uncompensated Care Pool is Used to Subsidize Medicaid," Forbes, http://www.forbes.com/sites/aroy/2011/05/18/massachusetts-uncompensated-care-pool-is-used-to-subsidize-medicaid/

blueprint for a government-run online insurance marketplace, or exchange."[169] Although Romneycare lowered the percentage of uninsured to 4.4% in 2012, problems and concerns remain.[170] One problem is that Romneycare has done little to control the ever-escalating costs of healthcare in Massachusetts. A second problem is that reform added a large number of formerly uninsured and uninsurable individuals, who have the potential to overwhelm the doctor supply. We can anticipate these same concerns with Obamacare, because the same problems exist (or are worse) in the country at large.

ROMNEYCARE: TOO LITTLE TO CONTROL COSTS

According to Ashish Jha, a health policy researcher and physician, the first concern is "that the bill did too little to control rising healthcare costs."[171] As shown in Figure 5–E, the per capita healthcare spending in Massachusetts is 15% higher than the national average, and they have the highest individual market premiums in the country.[172]

169 "The Massachusetts (health care) experiment," CNN, Jun 4, 2013, http://money.cnn.com/2013/06/01/pf/massachusetts-health-care.moneymag/index.html

170 Samuel Weigley, Alexander E.M. Hess, and Michael B. Sauter, "Doctor shortage could take turn for the worse," USA Today, Oct 2012, http://www.usatoday.com/story/money/business/2012/10/20/doctors-shortage-least-most/1644837/

171 "Did Massachusetts Healthcare Reform Hurt Access to Care for the Previously Insured?" http://blogs.sph.harvard.edu/ashish-jha/did-massachusetts-healthcare-reform-hurt-access-to-care-for-the-previously-insured/

172 Sarah Kliff, "Five facts about Obamacare and health premiums," Washington Post, http://www.washingtonpost.com/blogs/wonkblog/wp/2013/01/06/five-facts-about-obamacare-and-health-premiums/

Figure 5-E: The Per-Capita Healthcare Spending by State

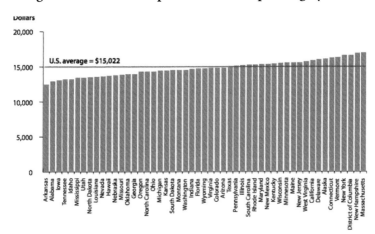

In fact, healthcare costs were so high, even after Romneycare, that Massachusetts pushed through Mass Health Reform 2.0 to moderate spending in four basic ways that bring Romneycare even closer to Obamacare: [173]

- set statewide healthcare spending growth caps

- promote new payment models

- encourage the development of accountable care organizations

- establish a health policy commission [174]

However, the jury is still out as to whether the 2.0 reform will be proven to be an effective cost control measure. Note that a survey conducted by the Massachusetts Medical Society in 2013,

---

173 Ashish Jha, "Did Massachusetts Health Care Reform Hurt Access To Care for the Previously Insured," The Health Care Blog, http://thehealthcareblog.com/blog/2013/03/05/did-massachusetts-health-care-reform-hurt-access-to-care-for-the-previously-insured/
174 Nancy Turnbull, "The Release Of Massachusetts Health Reform 2.0," Health Affairs Blog, Aug 2012, http://healthaffairs.org/blog/2012/08/13/the-release-of-massachusetts-health-reform-2-0/

shows that 78% of residents still find the cost of care to be the most important healthcare issue facing Massachusetts today. In addition, 65% of residents believed their healthcare cost went up from the year before. [175]

Romneycare: 400,000 Newly Insured in the Blink of an Eye

Dr. Jha continues, "The second concern was that bringing hundreds of thousands of new people on to the health insurance rolls without a commensurate increase in physician supply would overwhelm the state's supply of physicians."[176] The new law increased the number of insured individuals by 8%, or 400,000 newly insured residents, in the blink of an eye.

As you might expect, primary care doctors were overwhelmed. Compare the drop in primary care doctors accepting new patients from 70% in 2007 to 50% in 2011. Concurrently, only 43% of internists and 56% of family doctors accept Commonwealth Care, which is the heavily-subsidized middle class insurance program.[177]

Commensurate with the reduction in primary care doctors is the increase in the average wait time for a routine checkup:

- 41 days to see an OB/GYN

- 43 days to meet with a gastroenterologist

- 48 days to schedule an appointment with an internist[178]

175 "Focus on health reform," The Kaiser Family Foundation, May 2012, http://kaiserfamilyfoundation.files.wordpress.com/2013/01/8311.pdf
176 Jha, "Did Massachusetts Health Care Reform Hurt Access to Care for the Previously Insured."
177 "National Health Preview: RomneyCare's Bad Outcomes Keep Coming," Wall Street Journal, http://online.wsj.com/article/SB10001424052748703864204576313370527615288.html
178 Ibid.

There are those who believe that Massachusetts' healthcare reform is an "Obamacare Preview," furthering the view that we will get higher demand for insurance and healthcare services if the government subsidizes it.[179]

BUT WAIT: MASSACHUSETTS IS BETTER OFF THAN MOST OTHER STATES

Massachusetts was better prepared to serve its constituents before Romneycare than any other state will be coming into Obamacare. Massachusetts has always been a wealthy state with the highest ratio of physicians to patient care—315 doctors for every 100,000 residents—and the highest number of insured residents—87% even before Romneycare. Romneycare had a much smaller challenge than Obamacare will have in converting the uninsured to insured. Based on the 13% uninsured rate in a state with a population of approximately 6.5 million before Romneycare, Massachusetts would have had only about **845,000 uninsured** individuals to convert to insured.

Figure 5-F: Health Insurance Coverage of Adults 19-64, 2009-2010

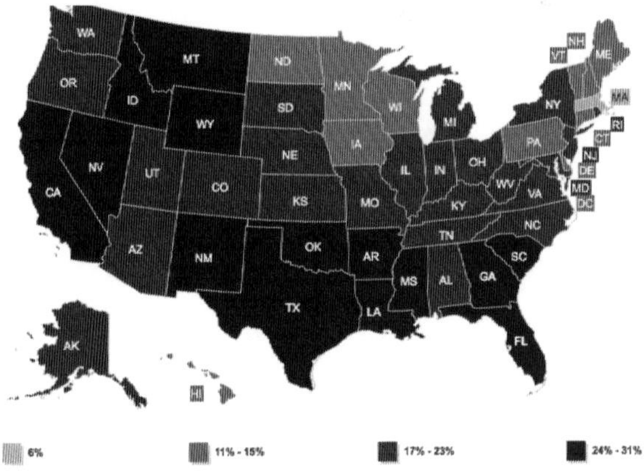

6%   11% - 16%   17% - 23%   24% - 31%

179 Ibid.

It follows that you can expect an even longer wait for service if you are in any other state than Massachusetts. With Obamacare, your state's healthcare system will be flooded with new, formerly uninsured and uninsurable patients. It is expected that the formerly uninsurable and underinsured individuals will seek treatment soon after they become insured; there is much pent-up demand from their lack of care in the past. As shown in Figure 5–F, consider that over 31% of Texans are uninsured today.[180] What can we expect when 4.8 million uninsured Texans come forward to claim their entitlement, with only about half the number of doctors available when compared to Massachusetts, to serve them under Obamacare?

States with doctor-to-patient ratios less than Massachusetts' will face a crisis. One example is Mississippi, which has the lowest doctor-to-patient ratio in the country—just 159 doctors for every 100,000 residents.[181] We can expect that the poorest states will be the most affected, similar to what we have seen in the U.K. and Canada.

Utah is another state that already faces problems in providing healthcare. Even though Utah is a wealthy state ($4,700 median household income higher than the national figure) it has only one medical school, and due to federal budget cuts, it was forced to reduce enrollment to 20 students per year. Making matters worse, Utah's population has been increasing. To keep up with demand, the state is trying to recruit out-of-state physicians to fill in the gap.[182]

Arkansas, with the third-lowest median household income in the U.S., is another state with severe problems. As the unhealthiest

---

180 Kaiser Foundation - Uninsured Adults Ages 19-64
181 "10 Sates with Most and Fewest Doctors," Wall Street Journal Market Watch, http://stream.marketwatch.com/story/markets/SS-4-4/SS-4-14886/
182 Ibid.

state in the country, Arkansas ranks 49th in its doctor-to-patient ratio. "In Arkansas 22.9% of adults smoked and 67.2% of adults were either overweight or obese."[183]

Georgia is one of the worst states for doctors looking to establish a successful practice. Even though enrollment in medical schools has increased by 50% in the last decade, "the state has just 20 doctors in a residency or fellowship program per 100,000 people, compared to the average of more than 35 per 100,000 people nationwide."[184] The median income is about $4,500 below the national average, and one out of five Georgians is uninsured, adding to the newly insured under Obamacare.

THE TAKEAWAY: LESSONS LEARNED

- Nationalized medicine has prevented Canada, the most highly educated country in the world, from attracting the doctors they need to care for their citizens.

- The drive for cost-efficiency in the U.K. has led to discrimination against certain classes, including the elderly, to cut procedures that might prolong life or improve the quality of life. Further, it has not led to universally good care in the U.K.

- Massachusetts, the state with highest physician ratio per capita, still needs more healthcare providers, and its healthcare costs are 15% higher than any other state.

---

183 Ibid.
184 Weigley et al., "Doctor Shortage Could Take a Turn for the Worst."

- Texas has introduced several interesting programs to keep up with the demand that their large population requires. Texas Tech offers attractive scholarships to first year medical students, something rare in medicine, to defray the average annual cost of medical school costs, which can be about $48,600.[185] Further, foreign-educated doctors are only required to work for three years in medically underserved areas in exchange for a Texas license. These doctors account for 24% of Texan doctors. Even with these extreme programs, Texas still has shortages in 36 out of 40 medical specialties, according to D Healthcare Daily.[186]

- If national healthcare causes broad shortages that hurt vulnerable populations, the rest of the nation is surely in trouble.

185 Ibid.
186 http://healthcare.dmagazine.com/2012/08/01/law-aimed-at-physician-shortages-may-make-them-worse-experts-say/

Chapter 6:

The Perfect Storm is Approaching - Accessing Care for Baby Boomers

"Rationing is inevitable in a world of finite resources."[187]

—Eduardo Porter, Journalist

The younger generations who must support the baby boomers, as our illustration[188] suggests, will certainly come to understand there are too few of them to support the perfect storm. No doubt you've heard about the escalating cost that comes with baby

---

187 "Rationing Healthcare More Fairly," NY Times, http://www.nytimes.com/2012/08/22/business/economy/rationing-health-care-more-fairly.html?pagewanted=all
188 The Grim Future Our Children Face; photo by rangizzz via Shutterstock.

boomers flooding the ranks of Medicare. Predictions of a bankrupt Medicare program in 2026 leave an uncertain future for the largest group of individuals to ever reach retirement age, as well as those younger workers who must support them. Demands for Medicare reductions abound and are already part of Obamacare's plans in the form of cuts to reimbursements for providers and institutions that service Medicare clients.

Times have certainly changed— it has not always been about cutting back. In 1965, President Lyndon Baines Johnson acknowledged Harry Truman's dream to remove the "financial barriers in the way of attaining  health" for all citizens, and seniors in particular, by signing both Medicare and Medicaid into law with the idea that "old folks are not going to be barred from a doctor's office or hospital because they don't have any money for medical attention." Of course the population of seniors in 1965 was only 19 million, and their life expectancy was five years less than that of seniors today. [189]

The Medicare Trustees Report issued the seventh-straight warning in 2013 that the Medicare Fund will be exhausted in 2026. One of only two public trustees, Charles Blahous III, believes that "Medicare costs are nearly certain to be higher than our current projections."[190] What drives Medicare costs?

---

189 Older Americans 2012, Key Indicators of Well-Being, Federal Interagency Forum on Aging-Related Statistics, Federal Interagency Forum on Aging Related Statistics, http://www.agingstats.gov/Main_Site/Data/2012_Documents/docs/EntireChartbook.pdf
190 Blahous, Charles, Mercatus Center, Expert Commentary: A Guide to the 2013 Medicare Trustees Report, http://mercatus.org/expert_commentary/guide-2013-medicare-trustees-report

- The increase in the sheer number of new beneficiaries to enroll in the next two decades—almost double since it began and expected to double again as baby boomers reach eligibility age (population projected to be 72 million by 2030) [191]

- The reduced population of younger workers who pay into the system, such as Social Security, will suffer because taxes on the wages of current workers pay for much of the expenses incurred by current beneficiaries, and there are simply fewer younger workers to pay for future beneficiaries.

- The unpredictability of the "healthcare cost inflation" based on improvements in life expectancy (longevity)[192]

- Better technology such as sophisticated scanning techniques, equipment to improve minimally invasive surgical techniques such as robotic equipment and improved surgical procedures and equipment where prosthetic devices are integrated with a patient's own brain

- The potential unsustainability of the aggressive Obamacare cuts to healthcare providers and hospitals

Why should you care about these predictions? Are they real, or is the situation even more grave? It is nearly impossible to jump on

---

191 Older Americans 2012, Key Indicators of Well-Being, Federal Interagency Forum on Aging-Related Statistics, Federal Interagency Forum on Aging Related Statistics, http://www.agingstats.gov/Main_Site/Data/2012_Documents/docs/EntireChartbook.pdf
192 Charles Blahous, "Expert Commentary: A Guide to the 2013 Medicare Trustees Report," Mercatus Center, http://mercatus.org/expert_commentary/guide-2013-medicare-trustees-report

the Obamacare information train at this point—it's already left the station and every political wonk is spinning their version along the tracks in an effort to tell you where they believe the Obamacare train is headed.

You will do well to squint a bit, to wade through the technical parts of this chapter since understanding the impact of this law and its policies and procedures may well make a difference in how long and how well you live. In order to try to clear the bureaucratic fog, you will find "Our View" boxes throughout this chapter that describe how we believe these complex policies might impact our senior clients. Here is how we will divide the topics in this chapter in order to present information you need to know about these complex issues:

> "Part I: The Problem with Medicare Funding—How the Doom and Gloom Predictions Are Only Part of the Picture" describes how Medicare works and why it's in trouble.

> "Part II: Strategies to Reduce Seniors' 'Overutilization' of Care" discusses some of the Obamacare changes that will directly affect how much care you may receive and how this helps.

> "Part III: How Does Uncle Sam Know the Best Course of Care for You?" describes some of the new agencies and committees that will oversee and advise your hospital and doctors about cost savings opportunities.

> "Part IV: Who's Paying the Piper? The Emerging Conflict of Interest in Post-Obamacare Medicine" challenges these strategies created for the medical community that can make a difference in how long and how well you live.

"Part V: The Effect of Medicare Reimbursement Cuts" discuss how the Medicare costs imposed by Obamacare will affect seniors and lead to less access to affordable care for Medicare recipients.

"Part VI: Take It or Leave It—Why Seniors Can't Just Buy Private Care" explores the difficult rules that physicians are required to follow with regards to treating Medicare patients and how the end result is really that seniors will be unable to simply buy private care from most physicians.

Be advised that the light at the end of the tunnel is likely a train and, yes, it could be a life or death situation. The implications are not theoretical. In the end, it is about you and your family.

PART I:
THE PROBLEM WITH MEDICARE FUNDING— HOW THE DOOM AND GLOOM PREDICTIONS ARE ONLY PART OF THE PICTURE

Medicare is the second-largest social insurance program in the U.S., spending over $574 billion in 2012. As a review, a summary of the Medicare plans is included in Figure 6–A.

Figure 6-A: Medicare Plans

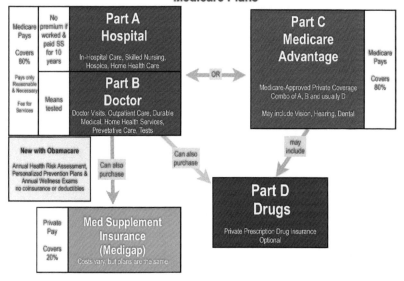

Every year, a board of trustees for the Hospitals Insurance Program, Part A, and the Supplementary Medical Insurance (SMI), Parts B and D, under Medicare submits a report to Congress on the financial health of Medicare. It is critical to understand that the Medicare Trustees' projections and warnings about the insolvency date are only part of the picture, even though the insolvency date is the major focus of the press and politicians. The insolvency date only reflects the health of the Hospital Insurance Trust Fund, Part A of Medicare, which is funded primary by payroll taxes. A greater worry to generations to come, however, should be the impact of SMI Trust Funds (Parts B and D) on the economy as a whole. SMI Trust Funds are not included in the projections of a solvency date because SMI is automatically provided for from the General Fund whenever there is a shortfall of SMI Trust Funds beyond taxes and premiums. Thus, the financial strains of SMI are a rising—and often overlooked—pressure on the general federal budget. Although most of us assume that Medicare Parts B and D are funded primarily by our premiums, that is simply not the case. Over 72% of Part B and 74% of Part D funding comes directly from general federal tax revenue as you can see in Figure 6–B.

Figure 6-B

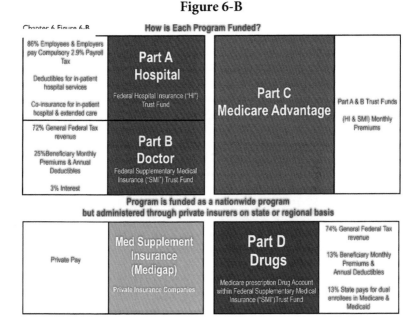

One way that Obamacare will help fund Part B in the future is by putting more of the burden to pay for Medicare on higher-income ($80,000/individual and $170,000/couple) beneficiaries. Most people pay more for care than the minimum $147 monthly deductible that the base rate for part B covers. Higher income beneficiaries pay 35–80% of the total premium resulting in premiums from $146.90 to $335.70 based on an increasing, sliding scale of annual income.[193] This threshold will stay the same through 2019; that is, it will not increase with inflation, meaning that more beneficiaries may reach the threshold and therefore pay more into

---

193 "Medicare 2013 costs at a glance," Medicare, http://www.medicare.gov/your-medicare-costs/costs-at-a-glance/costs-at-glance.html - collapse-4809

the Part B (SMI) Fund, relieving some of the burden on General Federal Tax Revenue funding.[194]

For one in four Medicare beneficiaries, healthcare consumes over 30% of their income.[195] Obamacare is certain to have a profound effect on the Medicare program and Medicare beneficiaries. To understand the effect, you must understand the Medicare-specific provisions of Obamacare.

PART II:
STRATEGIES TO REDUCE SENIORS' "OVERUTILIZATION" OF CARE

With so much high-pitched rhetoric and bureaucratic medicine-speak, it is difficult for most of us to understand the issues that will surely affect our care in the future. Here, we will attempt to present the issues and solutions related to overutilization, which has been identified as a major cause of escalating healthcare costs. Dr. Ezekiel Emanuel, President Obama's former healthcare advisor who is often identified as the architect of Obamacare, warned of a perfect storm that drives overutilization and increases the cost of care.[196] Note that Dr. Emanuel is the father of Rahm Emanuel, who was President Obama's White House Chief of Staff, so the influence of Dr. Emanuel on Obamacare should probably not be underrated. According to Dr. Emanuel, overutilization has two forms: (1) higher volumes of and (2) more costly specialists, tests, procedures, and prescriptions than are "appropriate."

---

194 "Medicare Spending and Financing Fact Sheet," The Kaiser Family Foundation, http:// kff.org/medicare/fact-sheet/medicare-spending-and-financing-fact-sheet/
195 Ibid.
196 "The Perfect Storm of Overutilization," JAMA (2008), http://jama.jamanetwork.com/ article.aspx?articleid=182076

Zebras Are Rarely Cost-Effective

"Zebras" are often blamed for higher volumes of costly specialists, tests, procedures, and prescriptions. What is a zebra? It is a rare disease that often presents with symptoms of a common disease. Among healthcare policy circles, there is a perceived bias that doctors see "zebras" in every case.[197] The origin of the zebra is an old saying that every medical student is taught to help them think logically about a differential diagnosis, "When you hear hoof beats, think of horses, not zebras," thereby directing them to look for the more commonplace rather than the more exotic explanation for an illness.

Figure 6–C: Is a Zebra Prudent or Overutilization?

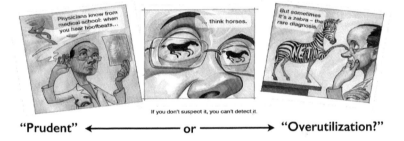

"Prudent" ←——————— or ——————→ "Overutilization?"

For example, a cough is generally the result of a commonplace virus (a horse), while tuberculosis would be a zebra. Dr. Emanuel admonishes medical schools for training doctors by "enumerating all possible diagnoses and tests that would confirm or exclude" rather than being training them to be "prudent." Obamacare will give payment preference to providers who use and report findings based on comparative research and evidence-based medicine,

---

197 Cartoon by Nikolay Gionov, Carcinoid Cancer encourages downloading to spread neuroendocrine tumor cancer, http://carcinoid.wordpress.com/2012/07/11/worldwide-net-cancer-awareness-day-alliance-launches-zebra-cartoon-sequel/

which are discussed later in this chapter. In other words, they will pay for horses, not zebras.

The concern is understandable, but you might have a very different opinion if your medical condition, or that of a loved one, is a zebra. For instance, consider Jenny, a 70-year-old diabetic with abdominal pain and nausea that is intermittent. What is the problem? As it does not appear life threatening, let's say we use the "new" method and reduce costs by having Jenny meet with a physician assistant, or PA, (a PA is not a doctor, but is trained to perform physical exams, diagnose and treat illnesses, order and interpret lab results, etc.). The PA gets out the government's evidence-based checklist of symptoms and determines that Jenny is probably just having a stomachache, so he prescribes a Nexium (the little purple pill) and sends Jenny home to rest. Later that day, Jenny has a heart attack and dies because the PA did not have the training or experience to understand that Jenny's symptoms are typical for a female diabetic in the early stages of a heart attack. It is likely that an experienced physician would have quickly discovered the problem and saved Jenny's life. The moral of the story is that there is a risk in basing diagnosis and treatment on generalized findings gleaned from research performed by individuals who are not physicians. They, and therefore their diagnoses, lack the training and the clinical experience that allow them to quickly sort out the zebras from the horses.

A practice founded on evidence-based medicine is often considered the cure for zebras. Evidence-based medicine is the "conscientious use of current best evidence in making decisions about the care of individual patients or the delivery of health services."[198] However, closer inspection may reveal that it is a double-edged sword. On the one hand, evidence-based medicine encourages doctors to make

---

198 "Evidence-based care and systemic reviews," The Cochrane Collaboration, http://www.cochrane.org/about-us/evidence-based-health-care

treatment decisions based on previous examples of effectiveness or ineffectiveness. On the other hand, individual cases are individual cases. That is why our culture values physicians so highly that it normally takes an additional 7 to 12 years of **post-graduate** training to license a physician. During this training they learn to spot the zebras and save lives. The problem is that the Center for Medicare and Medicaid Services (CMS) has closely linked evidence-based medicine to quality assurance measures and to a rationale for payment and, ultimately, cost savings. In a review of pros and cons, the American Society of Clinical Oncology states that, while evidence-based clinical practice guidelines are a credible source of data, they are "primarily designed as tools to broadly inform patient care rather than a roadmap for the treatment of a specific patient."[199]

> **OUR VIEW:** Zebras don't come along that often, but spotting one can make a substantial difference in the quality and length of life for the affected individual. Only a trained, experienced physician can spot an unusual condition easily and cost-effectively in order to save your life. Results of general studies, even those with thousands of subjects over many years still produce only general trends. While these studies can provide an experienced doctor with options for treatment, care, or education, there is no substitute for meeting with your physician so that your individual symptoms and situation are considered.

---

199 "Medicare's Coverage with Evidence Development: A Policy-Making Tool in Evolution," Journal of Oncology Practice, http://jop.ascopubs.org/content/3/6/296.full

A Group to Share Your Care Episodes

Fee-for-service was historically the way most physicians were paid by Medicare. Under the fee-for-service payment model, Medicare makes a direct payment to your doctor, surgeon, anesthesiologist, etc. Fee-for-service is another major cause of overutilization, according to Dr. Emanuel, because this type of payment to individual doctors creates an incentive for doctors to do more tests and procedures than they might do otherwise. Stated another way, fee-for-service payment rewards quantity—meaning overutilization by ordering more tests, more patient follow-ups, more treatments—over quality. He blames this payment system for driving up Medicare costs and therefore the federal deficit.

Dr. Emanuel also recommends a plan to move away from fee-for-service payment and toward bundled care payment models where healthcare organizations and hospitals, rather than individual doctors, will enter into "payment arrangements that include financial and performance accountability for episodes of care" (e.g. hip fracture or heart attack). Basically, when you have an "episode," Medicare will pay one check to your hospital, and the administrators at your hospital will decide *who* gets paid *how much* and *when*. Emanuel believes that using the bundled care model to pay for the treatment of patients is a better way to incentivize healthcare organizations than individual doctor fee-for-service payments. There are two points of view that are considered here. CMS deputy administrator Johnathan Blum assures us from the patient's point of view, that the bundled payment model encourages "hospitals, physicians, post-acute facilities, and other providers as applicable to work together to improve health outcomes and lower costs."[200] From the point of view of providers (this refers

---

200 "Though Obamacare Pays Less, Providers Flock to 'Bundled' Medicare Payments," Forbes, http://www.forbes.com/sites/brucejapsen/2013/02/01/though-obamacare-pays-less-medical-providers-flock-to-bundled-medicare-payments/

to hospitals and managed care groups), bundled care payment plans move away from fragmented care inherent in fee-for-service plans that leads to "poor coordination of patient care." This does, however, beg the question about the providers' conflict of interest in making healthcare organizations, rather than doctors, the entity that controls the payments.

Currently being tested are bundled care models that change the payment structure away from individual payments for individual doctor services and procedures as they are provided. The bundled care model prearranges payments with healthcare organizations (rather than individual doctors). The healthcare organizations pay affiliated doctors if they meet their standards for financial and performance accountability for care episodes.[201] The models being tested establish a target price for each type of care and include a variety of plans such as "care redesign and enhancements, such as reengineered care pathways using evidence-based medicine, standardized operating protocols, improved care transitions, and care coordination."[202] Models being tested now pay one payment to the hospital/health management group for all providers and procedures involved, and only after the "episode," not for each care provider for each procedure within the care event as it happens. Medicare beneficiaries can elect to receive care from one of the participating organizations, but CMS assures us that Medicare beneficiaries are not limited to who they choose as their healthcare provider. The idea here is that one lump sum payment is divided among all who participate in a patient's care "episode." This research project has initial funding for 5 years and includes 100 healthcare organizations. If CMS finds that these models reduce

---

201 "Bundled Payments for Care Improvement Initiative Fact Sheet," CMS, Jan 31, 2013, http://www.cms.gov/apps/media/press/factsheet PerPage=10&checkDate=&checkKey=& srchType=1&numDays=3500&srchOpt=0&srchData=&keywordType=All&chkNewsType =6&intPage=&showAll=&pYear=&year=&desc=&cboOrder=date
202 Ibid.

costs while not reducing quality of care, then they have the option to expand the program.[203]

What does this mean for seniors with chronic illnesses? One 28-year veteran family care physician, Dr. Bruce Bagley, wonders whether the family physician will be on equal footing with others on the proposed healthcare team since the hospital or healthcare organization determines how payments will be made proportional to perceived value contributed. As non-hospital employees, will primary care doctors be slowly phased out and replaced with non-physicians that are less expensive? [204]

You may have already experienced medicine delivered through healthcare teams if you have experience with a loved one in a nursing home. Generally, you are called to a "family meeting" to discuss the course of treatment with a team, usually led by a social worker and the nursing home care coordinator and consisting of nurses, physical therapists, speech therapists, and occupational therapists, but rarely a doctor. Recommendations for care are made by the "team" and not by a trained physician. Think about it: how often did your doctor visit at the nursing home? My personal experience with my mother-in-law was that her primary physician for over 20 years visited the nursing home every other week. Furthermore, no other physicians were at the facility regularly enough to identify and react to problems she had (including, at different times, numbness, hallucinations, aches, and pains).

> **OUR VIEW**: Bundled care arrangements put the hospital bean counters in control of your care. The incentives are just wrong—it rewards cost cutting over quality of care by virtue of disincentivizing and reducing control by your

---

203 "Medicare Bundled Payment Initiative Stretches from Coast to Coast," AAFP, http://www.aafp.org/news-now/practice-professional-issues/20130416bundledpayinitiative.html
204 Ibid.

physician. A team approach works only if a physician leads the team, a physician who sees actually sees you personally and regularly. To what degree can you trust a system to give you the proper tests and to offer options and treatment when the caregivers are incentivized to take the "most cost-effective" approach?

OVERUTILIZATION AND ESCALATING HEALTHCARE COSTS

Dr. Emanuel warns the leaders of medicine in the U.S. about the gravity of escalating healthcare costs and urges them toward "more socially sustainable, cost-effective care." Dr. Emanuel offers suggestions that we are seeing now in Obamacare: altering how insurance pays for medical services, more value-based co-payments, i.e., increased payments for more-effective and less-costly alternatives. We can see that Dr. Emanual's recommendations influence much of today's thinking about developing better—meaning more cost-effective—ways to incentivize doctors and hospitals. However, more cost-effective may not always mean better care. Consider that some procedures not only extend life but also improve quality of life. For example, the U.S. performs twice as many knee replacements as any European Union country, which of course drives up our healthcare-relative expenditures.[205] But do we really want to cut the knee replacements back? Does anyone check in for a knee surgery that they do not feel they need? Rather, our experience is that individuals finally submit to knee surgery as a last resort when they can no longer endure the pain. One alternative to knee surgery is to medicate for the pain, to "treat the symptoms," but what does this do to the individual's quality of life?

---

205 Nick J. Tate, The Obamacare Survival Guide, 122–123.

Reducing Overutilization with Competitive Bidding

In a New York Times editorial, Dr. Emanuel describes the promise of competitive bidding that will be required beginning in 2016 for items such as oxygen equipment, wheelchairs, and diabetic testing equipment.[206] CMS promises that the new program will pay "lower, more accurate prices." AARP describes the competitive bidding program as one that is designed to reduce the waste and fraud that forced Medicare to pay three to four times what commercial insurers paid for the same equipment and supplies. From a practical point of view, the program will change how you purchase equipment and supplies.[207] For instance, if you are in one of the areas where the program is in place, you must use a Medicare-approved supplier. Further, if you are a diabetic, you must use their mail-order contract supplier for testing supplies or a store or pharmacy that accepts Medicare-approved payment as payment in full. If your doctor prescribes a specific brand or form of equipment and supplies, he or she will be required to put a note to justify the specific recommendation in your medical record. Then, a Medicare-approved contract supplier is required to either furnish that brand or form, help you find another contract supplier who can, or work with your doctor to find a safe and effective alternative. Even now, doctors must argue with insurance companies for hours to authorize treatments they know are superior for their patients. Faced with an ever-increasing caseload, physicians have less and less time to fight for their patients than insurance companies have to fight for their "savings." This will only get worse once more solid financial lines are drawn.

---

206 "Health Care Good News," New York Times, http://opinionator.blogs.nytimes.com/2013/02/14/health-cares-good-news/
207 "Money-Saving Changes Come to Medicare," AARP, http://www.aarp.org/health/medicare-insurance/info-06-2013/medicare-competitive-bidding-program.html

> **OUR VIEW**: Competitive bidding makes sense, but there is as much room for abuse and waste as there is without it. Restrictions that require you to use a "safe and effective alternative" will delay the process of getting the treatment you need while begging the question about who (the doctor or the contractor) will make the final decision. We feel certain that more doctors will simply give up trying to get you what they feel is superior treatment due to the bureaucratic hassles involved in the process.

PART III:
HOW DOES UNCLE SAM KNOW THE BEST COURSE OF CARE FOR YOU?

Medicare struggles to develop programs that require the healthcare community to provide beneficiaries with care that is cost-effective and appropriate. Informed decisions, evidence-based medicine, patient-centered outcomes, comparative effective research, and many other new-age sounding terms make it difficult to follow the direction of new Obamacare initiatives. In this section, we will review some of the organizations and evaluation models that will direct the course of medical care for all, but particularly for seniors.

Patient-Centered Outcomes Research Institute (PCORI)

A new nonprofit, non-governmental organization will play a central role under Obamacare in developing and funding comparative effectiveness research to "assist patients, clinicians, purchasers, and policy-makers in making informed health decisions."[208] Patient-Centered Outcomes Research Institute (PCORI) is funded by Medicare dollars and a fee that has been added to private insurance. PCORI is governed by the Government Accountability Office and by presidential appointees of the National Institutes of Health and the Agency for Healthcare Research and Quality. A major initiative within PCORI is to disseminate research findings regarding relative health outcomes, clinical effectiveness, and the appropriateness of medical treatment and services. The "comparative effectiveness" is intended to compare the benefits, risks, and effectiveness of two or more treatments or services for the same condition. Although the comparative research may be beneficial in reviewing alternatives and discussing options with patients, at least some experts believe that it should be only a part of the decision-making process that should include physician's training and experience as well as the patient's values and preferences.[209]

A question is whether comparative research recommendations will limit the options available to seniors. Think about someone you know whose life has been improved because of an expensive treatment that might not be the first choice according to comparative effectiveness research. One of our clients, whom we will call John, found out that he had prostate cancer. Rather than

---

208 Protection and Affordable Care Act of 2010 § 6301(a) (codified as amended at 42 U.S.C. § 1320e(b)(1))
209 "Comparative Effectiveness Research Under Obamacare: A Slippery Slope to Health Care Rationing," The Heritage Foundation, http://www.heritage.org/research/reports/2012/04/comparative-effectiveness-research-under-obamacare-a-slippery-slope-to-health-care-rationing

blindly accepting the normal surgical procedures that often cause incontinence and erectile dysfunction, his physician suggested proton therapy. The operation was performed at a small private clinic at the cost of $180,000. When we saw John in our office, he was cancer-free with no side effects. So, what would the comparative research recommend, and what might that suggest about whether Medicare would pay for a patient to receive proton therapy? The answer is unknown, as there have not been enough studies conducted to know. One researcher from the Agency for Healthcare Research and Quality, part of the National Institutes of Health, discusses the lack of clinical evidence that suggests proton therapy as superior for prostate cancer, but rather that it is strongest "for . . . tumors surrounded by critical structures such as the eye, brain and spinal cord."[210] Because of this, CMS has not issued a national coverage or noncoverage determination for proton beam therapy in prostate cancer.

> **OUR VIEW**: We believe that most men would agree that prostate cancer affects a "critical structure" and deserves the greatest possible consideration for treatment. Once again, results from studies should be used as a guideline, not a roadmap for individual treatment.

Beyond conducting comparative studies, PCORI establishes the priorities for the national research agenda and has broad-ranging authority to investigate new evidence that may improve health outcomes and the quality of care, in addition to affecting national healthcare expenditures. They are charged with influencing patients and clinicians in making informed health decisions. PCORI will have access to the data networks from Medicare, Medicaid, and Children's Health Insurance Programs, as well as

---

210 Stephanie Jarosek, Sean Elliott, and Beth A Virnig, "Proton beam radiotherapy in the U.S. Medicare population: growth in use between 2006 and 2009" Data Points 10 (Rockville, MD: 2012), http://www.ncbi.nlm.nih.gov/books/NBK97147/

public and private entities so that they can complete comparative research. It follows that the foremost recommendations will affect seniors since there has been so much data collected for them. Interestingly, private and university research programs have to pay hefty fees for this same data, which often hinders its use in these settings for research. This means that almost all recommendations for treatment guidelines will be coming from one source, and that source is also being funded by the entity paying for your healthcare.

Of course, PCORI can appoint as many permanent or ad hoc expert advisory panels as they feel are necessary. Evidence-based medicine, integrative health and primary prevention strategies are a priority.

THE INDEPENDENT PATIENT ADVISORY BOARD (IPAB)

The Independent Patient Advisory Board or IPAB is one of the many advisory boards created by Obamacare that has garnered much scrutiny and media attention. Facts about its purpose and operation have been obscured by the emotional nature of the political discussion. In order to clearly explore what the IPAB means to seniors, this section will answer basic questions about what it is, how it works, and the impact it will have on seniors.

What is the IPAB? The IPAB is a 15-member committee that uses a spending target system and fast-track legislative approval to get the job done.

What is the purpose of the IPAB? The stated purpose of the IPAB is to "reduce the per capita rate of growth in Medicare spending."[211]

---

211 42 USC §1395kkk(b) (2012).

At the same time, IPAB is charged to maintain quality and access without raising out-of-pocket costs for Medicare beneficiaries.

Who is on the IPAB? The IPAB members can be physicians, healthcare practitioners, consumer representatives, and seniors, however the majority must be NON-providers. They are appointed to six-year terms by the president and approved by the Senate.[212]

How does it work? Every year, an actuarial projection of the per capita spending growth rate—a target growth rate—is prepared by the Centers for Medicare and Medicaid Services (CMS). Then, the CMS actuaries determine whether the projected growth rate will exceed the target in the next two years. If the projected exceeds the target, then IPAB proposes recommendations for Congress. Congress has until August 15th each year to pass a bill of their own, which must be passed with a super majority, to achieve the proposed savings, or IPAB's recommendations will automatically take effect.[213] This is set to begin on January 15, 2014.

Figure 6–D: Setting the Target Growth Rate

2013
Determination
Will Implementation-year estimates exceed Target Growth?

2014
Proposal
IPAB issues proposals to reach Target Growth

2015
Implementation
IPAB proposal is law unless Congress passes a low with > savings

212 "Health Care Reform: Congress creates Independent Advisory Board," OrthopedicsToday, http://www.healio.com/orthopedics/business-of-orthopedics/news/print/orthopedics-today/%7Bbf3ee47b-5929-40a6-9d1a-8b76 a
213 "Independent Payment Advisory Board," AMA, http://www.ama-assn.org/resources/doc/washington/ipab-summary.pdf

Why is there so much controversy about the IPAB? Two major issues surround the IPAB. First, it is not an advisory board—their proposals will become law unless Congress acts with an alternate proposal that saves at least as much as the IPAB proposal would have saved.

Second, IPAB does have advisors such as MedPAC (explained later in this chapter) who can recommend cuts. It is likely IPAB will take into account these recommendations since the majority of the committee members are not subject-matter (i.e. medical) experts. IPAB proposals affecting hospitals and skilled nursing facilities will not be implemented until 2020, but physician and supplier cuts can start in 2015. Contrary to some statements made about IPABs, they are expressly forbidden to ration healthcare; raise revenues; raise Medicare beneficiary premiums; or increase deductibles, coinsurance, or copays.

> **OUR VIEW**: The big question is this: How can the IPAB possibly succeed in maintaining access and quality of medical care without raising costs? Although there may be some fraud, overuse, etc., in the current system, at some point the overwhelming number of baby boomers and their illnesses as they age are likely to overwhelm the system with cost. Do you think that you will receive more or less care? Do you think you will receive better or worse care?

PART IV:
WHO'S PAYING THE PIPER? THE EMERGING CONFLICT OF INTEREST IN POST-OBAMACARE MEDICINE

Medicare is the largest single purchaser of healthcare in the US, accounting for 23%, or $522 billion, of the dollars spent on overall healthcare. There are over 165 provisions in Obamacare that directly affect the Medicare program, and many feel that physicians will be the hardest hit by Obamacare.[214] The

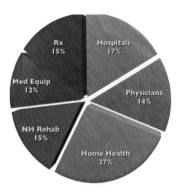

Figure 6-E: Medicare Spending

Medicare Payment Advisory Commission, or MedPAC, is yet another independent commission that is charged with reporting to Congress on Medicare fee-for-service payments systems, the Medicare Advantage program, and the prescription drug program. They report the impact of Medicare on GDP and the federal budget, evaluate the adequacy of the payment systems, and make recommendations regarding payment for most Medicare services.[215] In their 2013 report, they note that Medicare spending among fee-for-service beneficiaries has increased significantly since 2002 across all sectors (hospital inpatient, physician, post-acute, hospital outpatient, inpatient psychiatric hospital, and Ambulatory Surgical Centers).[216] As might be expected, they report that the costliest beneficiaries tend to be those with chronic conditions who account for about 1% of the total number of

---

214 "Obamacare's Impact on Doctors," The Heritage Foundation, http://www.heritage.org/research/reports/2013/08/obamacares-impact-on-doctors-an-update
215 "Report to the Congress: Medicare Payment Policy," Medpac, (Mar 2011) http://www.medpac.gov/documents/Mar11_EntireReport.pdf
216 "Medpac Data Book," (2013) http://www.medpac.gov/documents/Jun13DataBookEntire Report.pdf

Medicare fee-for-service beneficiaries. MedPAC focuses on fee-for-service because Medicare spends close to 40% of its budget on the most costly 5% of beneficiaries and only 5% on the least costly 50%. Beneficiaries with end-stage renal disease (ESRD) incur six times greater spending than those without ESRD. While Medicare spent about $10,500 on the average beneficiary, close to $70,000 was spent on each ESRD beneficiary.

There is much at stake for President Obama and for many generations to come. Obamacare is already implementing programs to incentivize hospitals to improve care and reduce costly readmissions. We will discuss these programs as well as the unintended ethical implications they may present to physicians. Will they spend more but ultimately save less?

CMS's Carrot and Stick for Physicians—Outcomes-Based Bonuses and Penalties

CMS has initiated a program to revamp the way healthcare services are paid for so that better value, better outcomes, and innovations are rewarded rather than volume.[217] The Hospital Value-based Purchasing Program will immediately link nearly $1 billion in payments to 3,000 hospitals, based on the quality of care provided to patients.[218] Hospitals will be compared based on how reliably they meet rudimentary standards of care and the ratings from patients regarding responsiveness and communications with doctors and nurses. Medicare is paying for this program

---

217 "Medicare Quality Initiatives Patient Assessment Instruments Presentation," CMS, http://www.cms.gov/Medicare/Quality-Initiatives-Patient-Assessment-Instruments/HospitalQualityInits/Downloads/0210_Slides.pdf
218 "Medicare Discloses Hospitals' Bonuses, Penalties Based on Quality," Kaiser Health News (Dec 20, 2012) http://www.kaiserhealthnews.org/stories/2012/december/21/medicare-hospitals-value-based-purchasing.aspx

by reducing payments to all hospitals by 1% ($948 million) and then reallocating the 1% among the winners. In the first year of the payments, as a penalty for poor performance, nearly half will lose the 1% they contributed.[219] The winners and losers say that it is insignificant to their budgets. However, it seems obvious that it does have the potential for real impact on their status (or not) within the industry. Also, it seems likely that potential patients will check out their ratings that are published and publicly available on the Internet and in press releases. Medicare will make incentive payments based on:

- Achievement: How well the hospital performs on quality measures compared to an average of all hospitals' baseline period performance.

- Improvement: How much improvement the hospital has made, based on its own performance during a baseline period.

The higher their performance on either of these measures, the higher their value-based incentive payments will be. Deficient or small hospitals are excluded from the program. 70% of the incentives are based on 17 clinical process measures that appear to be done/not-done type items, such as aspirin prescribed at discharge, discharge instructions provided, and pneumococcal vaccination given. 30% of the incentives are more "soft" and include areas such as nurse communication, doctor communication and hospital staff responsiveness. Further, hospitals can earn "consistency points" if all of their scores are equal to or greater than the achievement threshold. All of this information will be published on the Hospital Compare website.

---

219 Ibid.

What does this mean for physicians? The presumption in these new rules is that physicians add tests, procedures, and other services to boost the quantity and complexity of services to seniors and thus increase the hospital's fee-for-service compensation. It is more likely that these additional services result from a fear of malpractice rather than physicians consciously boosting their fees by ordering more tests. The question remains whether doctors will respond to the change in pay based on this new program if there is not a concurrent change in the threat of malpractice. Interestingly, the insurance industry seems to feel that Obamacare could decrease malpractice because more people will enter the healthcare system younger and get care earlier in life, before conditions are more permanent. Thereby, these patients may be more easily treated with less chance for error or speculation about error. [220]

Another issue for doctors is the reductions in fees generally (hospitals receive 71% and doctors 81% of private pay rates) from Medicare with this bonus/penalty program added on top. Dr. Jason Foder of the Galen Institute opines, "These underpayments are ultimately shifted to patients in the form of shorter visits, less doctor face time, quick hospital discharges, and compromised care.[221] Dr. Foder is not impressed by the amount of additional paperwork and documentation required by Obamacare that takes away, in his opinion, from patient care. He feels that these underpayments are passed on to private pay patients. He worries that the sickest, most complicated patients may find it difficult to find care because they have the potential to raise a doctor's costs by requiring more tests, consults, and procedures to deal with their conditions.

---

220 "How Obamacare could affect P/C Insurance," Insurance Journal, http://www. insurancejournal.com/news/national/2013/03/28/286243.htm

221 Jason Fodeman, "The New Health Law: Bad for Doctors, Awful for Patients," The Institute for Health Care Consumerism, http://www.theihcc.com/en/communities/policy_legislation/the-new-health-law-bad-for-doctors-awful-for-patie_gn17y01k.html

> OUR VIEW: On the one hand, these new performance measures will create more transparency and incentives for hospitals and physicians to take care of the basics and provide a better care experience for patients. On the other hand, it seems likely that the inherent bureaucracy will also negatively impact how we interact with our physicians.

MORE VALUE-BASED PURCHASING PENALTIES: THE HOSPITAL READMISSIONS REDUCTION PROGRAM

Twenty percent of Medicare patients are readmitted to a hospital within one month of discharge, which CMS feels is excessive and indicates that patients are not getting the quality of care they should expect.[222] As part of their Value-Based Purchasing Program, CMS initiated a penalty program beginning in 2012 for hospitals with excess readmission. The purpose of the program is to make sure that hospitals discharge patients when they are fully prepared and will be safe at home or at a facility. As with the measures in the Value-Based Purchasing Program, the purpose is to reward quality and not just quantity of medical care to Medicare beneficiaries. The penalty for excess readmissions is a direct and *escalating* reduction in payment of up to 2% in 2013 and 3% in 2014 of every payment to hospitals who accept Medicare patients. The problem with this approach is that the penalty is not just associated with the costs of excess readmissions; rather it is a penalty on a*ll Medicare payments* that a problem hospital receives.[223] While it is likely that this draconian penalty will certainly make hospitals more careful

---

222 "Medicare's Hospital Readmission Reduction FAQ," http://www.acep.org/Legislation-and-Advocacy/Practice-Management-Issues/Physician-Payment-Reform/Medicare-s-Hospital-Readmission-Reduction-Program-FAQ/
223 Ibid

about prematurely discharging payments, it is also more likely to make hospitals more reluctant to readmit patients.

Medicare will levy fines of $227 million in 2013 to hospitals across the country. The Hospital Readmission Reduction Program tracks patients who are readmitted within a certain time frame from discharge. The readmission rates for the 2,217 hospitals in the program are compared and adjusted for certain factors such as demographics and patient frailty. Through 2015, the conditions included are limited to heart attacks, heart failure, or pneumonia, but additional conditions may to be added based on MedPAC (the independent reporting agency that reports on Medicare costs Congress) recommendations.

CMS is encouraging hospitals to use non-doctors in the process. Nurses, case managers, and discharge planners are brought in to assess high-risk patients prior to discharge and set up a plan for each. Hospitals are also expected to take measures such as coordinating with community resources such as physicians and home health agencies to assure that the patient understands the plan and has access to the prescriptions and information they might need to reduce the chance for readmission. Emergency physicians will be expected to work with hospital case managers and discharge planners to determine if there is a safe, alternative care setting for the patient.

There are problems and questions about the program from the medical community. First, there is a question about the reliability of the measures across different hospital populations. For instance, hospitals with a large number of low-income patients were more likely to be penalized.[224] Unlike other measures in the Value-Based

224 "Armed With Bigger Fines, Medicare To Punish 2,225 Hospitals for Excess Readmissions," Kaiser Health News, http://www.kaiserhealthnews.org/Stories/2013/August/02/readmission-penalties-medicare-hospitals-year-two.aspx

Purchasing Program, there is no reward for improvement, nor is there a way to opt out. Second, there is a question about whether hospitals that treat populations with more complex problems will be targeted. Medicare counters that they do not need to take socioeconomic factors into account because they have factored in differing health of these populations. Third, hospitals are concerned that the penalties will impact care for low-income patients who have a harder time understanding and carrying out post-hospital instructions. Typically, they readmit low-income patients who are not healing because they cannot afford costly medications or stick with an expensive low-salt diet.

Medicare officials believe that this penalty will remove the incentive that rewards hospitals if their patients' health deteriorates after they are discharged, because a readmission is a second payment. MedPAC believes that Medicare can save $1 billion. Hospitals will be fined for each patient stay, so readmitted patients will cause their fines to be higher—up to $1 million in 2012 for a large hospital. [225]In a strange twist, hospitals that improve may actually have less revenue because they would forego the second admission.

Readmissions are a costly problem for Medicare. Hospitals are clearly focused on the problem and have ramped up their efforts to communicate better with patients through discharge planning. The worry is that patients with more complex problems or a less supportive environment in which to go after discharge will in some way be treated differently.

> **OUR VIEW**: While excess-readmission penalties may seem like a good idea, the policy may have unintended consequences. In coping with all of the financial disincentives, hospitals—and the doctors who are in increasing numbers employed by hospitals—will be

225 Ibid

less likely to work with complex problem cases, such as a widow with diabetes and a heart condition who lives alone. That could be you or me or someone you know. What will you do to ensure access?

In addition, since readmitting patients within one month will be extremely punitive to a hospital, we feel certain that there will be pressure on the skilled nursing facilities that benefit from hospital referrals to keep the patient rather than send them back to the hospital for readmission. This policy may very well result in higher death rates in these skilled nursing facilities without the proper hospital care that a readmission would allow. The incentives here just seem wrong to us.[226]

PART V:
THE EFFECT OF MEDICARE REIMBURSEMENT CUTS

The $716 billion reduction in Medicare payments for healthcare providers will take place over the next decade. Most cuts are expected to come from reductions in fraud, waste, and abuse. CMS projects that Obamacare will reduce the projected spending rate from 6.8% to 5.3% for a 10-year savings of $575 billion.[227] The plans to reduce the overall growth rate of Medicare depend on the success of a wide range of programs. Some we have discussed in previous parts of this chapter, but there are more.

---

226 "Hospice 2014 Final Rule on Payment, Quality, Coding and Hospice in Nursing Homes," LeadingAge, http://www.leadingage.org/LeadingAge_Comments_Hospice_2014_ Proposed_Rule.aspx. Note that CMS is increasing Hospice Care by 1% in 2014.
227 "Affordable Care Act Update: Implementing Medicare Cost Savings," CMS, http://www. cms.gov/apps/docs/aca-update-implementing-medicare-costs-savings.pdf

Cost Containment: For Every CMS Action, There Is a Market Reaction

Figure 6–F: Cost Containment Strategies from CMS

Cost Containment Strategy	Key Provisions	10-Year Cost Savings in Billions
A. Improve Quality of Care	1. Reduce hospital readmissions 2. Reduce conditions acquired in the hospital 3. Bundle payments 4. Improve physician quality reporting	$8.2 $3.2 $1.7 $1.9
B. Reform Delivery System	1. Promote Accountable Care Organizations 2. Establish the IPAB	$4.9 $23.7
C. Appropriately Price Services and Modernize Financing Systems	1. End Medicare Advantage Overpayments 2. Improve productivity and market basket adjustments in most provider settings 3. Modify advanced imaging service payments 4. Expand Durable Medical competitive bidding	$145 $205 $2.0 $1.7
D. Fight Waste, Fraud, and Abuse	A variety of measures, such as: ■ Expanding Recovery Audit ■ ContractorsRequiring face encounters with physicians before receiving certain services ■ Requiring greater data matching capabilities	$4.9

We have already discussed most of the cost containment strategies outlined above. Now, we will look at changes to the Medicare Advantage programs that will have a far-reaching reaction from the marketplace. We will also discuss Obamacare's impacts to physicians.

Medicare Advantage—Funding Reductions Means Fewer Choices for Seniors

Medicare Advantage accounts for 22% of Medicare spending.[228] The first Medicare Advantage plan, or Medicare+Choice plan

228 "Medicare Advantage Fact Sheet," The Kaiser Family Foundation, http://kff.org/medicare/fact-sheet/medicare-advantage-fact-sheet/

as it was originally named, rolled out in January 1999 based on directives from the Balanced Budget Act of 1997. CMS is authorized to offer private health plans, mainly through health maintenance organizations (HMOs) and preferred provider organizations (PPOs) as an alternative to regular Medicare Part A and B, including a separate payment for Part D. **The payment policy for plans has shifted from savings to expanding plans and providing extra plans to enrollees, which has resulted in Medicare Advantage costing more than traditional Medicare.**

Now, Obamacare will bring spending back in line with the original cost-savings goals over a period of time. In addition, Medicare will offer bonus payments to plans based on quality ratings and require that these plan maintain a medical loss ratio of at least 85%.[229] Originally, there was a per-enrollee cost for the services bidding process, and, in more rural areas, a benchmark was set locally or regionally. The benchmark established what Medicare paid and what individuals paid. If the plan bid is higher, then enrollees pay the difference (in addition to their Part A/B premiums). If it's lower, then the plan and Medicare split the difference between the bid and the benchmark. The plan's share of the payment is known as a rebate, and it must be used to provide supplemental benefits, such as dental care and glasses, to enrollees. Obamacare also changed the reimbursement method to reduce the benchmarks over a period of time, but it allows plans with higher-quality ratings to keep a larger share of the rebate. All plans limit beneficiaries' out-of-pocket spending to no more than $6,700.

The Kaiser Family Foundation suggests that the outlook for Medicare Advantage Plans will depend on several critical factors that have the potential to limit choices for enrollees by increasing out-of-pockets costs and access. These factors include:

- Location of the plans, e.g., rural plans tend to be more expensive

---

229 Ibid.

- Historical commitment to the Medicare market

- Ability to leverage efficiencies in delivering care to enrollees

- Potential quality ratings and therefore their ability to obtain bonuses

If you are a Medicare Advantage enrollee, you have heard a lot about cuts to the program. The Affordable Care Act actually included two parts, the Patient Protection and Affordable Care Act of 2010 (sometimes called PPACA) and a second bill, the Health Care and Education Reconciliation Act of 2010 (HCERA) that has implications for Medicare Advantage enrollees. HCERA imposes spending requirements for healthcare and quality-improvement efforts beginning in 2014.[230] Choice and access are the biggest potential losses for enrollees. Many providers are forced to move out of the Medicare Advantage market because they cannot maintain a profit in the face of the CMS's growing list of costly quality-related requirements, a reduction of $156 billion in Medicare Advantage payments over the next decade, the overall 2% reduction in Medicare spending required by the Budget Control Act of 2011, and any other spending cuts that seem imminent from Congress. These prompted the CEO of United Healthcare to say:

> "The depth of the underfunding of these benefits to seniors is causing us to exit certain market areas, reduce the number of plan offerings and reduce benefits in the majority of the local markets we serve commensurate with our review of the competitive position and long-term sustainability of our services for each individual market."[231]

230 Allison Bell, "CMS Sets Medicare Advantage and drug plan MLR rules," Life Health Pro, http://www.lifehealthpro.com/2013/05/20/cms-sets-medicare-advantage-and-drug-plan-mlr-rule

231 Matt Dunning, "Large health insurers plan to make cuts to their Medicare Advantage programs," Business Insurance, http://www.businessinsurance.com/article/20130825/NEWS03/308259985?tags=|307|74|82

There are also examples of this already happening. In 2010, Harvard Pilgrim Health Care dropped out of Medicare Advantage. The result was that their 22,000 enrollees were forced to look elsewhere for benefits. Lynn Bowman, vice president at Harvard Pilgrim, discussed the decision to exit the market:

> "We became concerned by the long term viability of Medicare Advantage programs in general. We know that cuts in Medicare are being used to fund national healthcare reform. And we also had concerns about our ability to build a network of healthcare providers that would meet the needs of our seniors."[232]

OUR VIEW: The future of Medicare Advantage programs is uncertain. Enrollees who may have enjoyed extra benefits in the past will surely find that their provider choices and benefits are reduced as insurers flee the market in response to the government's drive to reduce costs and increase quality. As is often suggested, there is no direct reduction to Medicare beneficiaries, but the collateral damage of reductions to the providers will have far-reaching negative impacts on Medicare enrollees. While we think that it is too early to make client recommendations related to Medicare Advantage programs, we are watching this area closely to determine whether our clients might want to switch from their current Advantage Plans back to private Medicare supplement programs, should they face reduced benefits or access to care.

---

232 Nick J. Tate, The Obamacare Survival Guide, 144.

Your Physician at the Bottom of the Obamacare Barrel

"The majority of physicians believe health reform will increase their patient loads while decreasing the financial viability of their practices."

—The Physicians Foundation

The Physicians Foundation is a not-for-profit organization that is dedicated to advancing the work of practicing physicians and to improving the healthcare of all Americans. In a recent publication, their experts revealed some of the impacts of Obamacare. If you have or wish to have a personal relationship with your physician in the future, this will be of interest to you.

Figure 6–G: Your Future with Your Physician [233]

What the Report Said	What It Could Mean to You
Obamacare, unlike previous reform healthcare efforts will "usher in substantive and lasting changes."	Obamacare is not going away, regardless of what the politicians say.
"The independent, private physician practice model will be largely, though not uniformly, replaced."	Your doctor will not be a "local" doctor anymore.
Most physicians will be compelled to become part of a larger organization—consolidated with other doctors or as a hospital employee—for capital, administrative and technical resources.	Was your local bank acquired by a larger bank? This is the same idea in the medical field.
Physicians will spend more time on compliance. "Reform will drastically increase physician legal compliance and potential liability under federal fraud and abuse statues."	More paperwork means less time for you and more expense, which may be passed to you, for your doctor.
Reform will "exacerbate physician shortages, creating access issues for many patients." It follows that, given a choice, many will opt out of private practice or abandon medicine altogether.	Obamacare will require your doctor to see more patients at less cost with increased paperwork. There will be doctor shortages.
The Sustainable Growth Rate (SGR) formula, which would cut physician payments by 23%, will be a problem that Congress will not fix. New payment mechanisms will make it more difficult for physicians.	The way your doctor is paid will change. Their piece of the payment pie will be reduced substantially while the quality standards they must meet increase. This presents a dilemma.

233 Health Reform and the Decline of Physician Private Practice: A White Paper Examining the Effects of the Patient Protection and Affordable Care Act on Physician Practices in the United States, The Physician's Foundation (Merritt Hawkins: 2010).

Fewer and fewer physicians are working with and paid by patients one-on-one. As you can clearly see in Figure 6–H, less than one-third of doctors today work in one- or two-physician practices. Rather, physicians are joining groups who can better negotiate with insurers and the government for payment. Historically, hospitals were seen as an extension of the doctors' practice and shared the authority to provide care to patients. Physicians were responsible for clinical care of the individual patient and policed themselves through peer credentialing. Hospital administrators oversaw operational matters to meet needs at the community level, providing a place for treating patients and the technology and support staff that the physicians required. A wave of managed care initiatives that began in the 1990s were an effort to integrate hospitals with physicians to gain bargaining power, but the initiatives lacked the buy-in from physicians and lacked management expertise from hospitals. More recent attempts, including Obamacare pilots, have focused on developing better quality metrics and rewarding efficiency.

Figure 6-H: US Physicians by Practice Type

U.S. PHYSICIANS BY PRACTICE TYPE

32% Solo/2-Physician Practice
15% Group Practice, 3-5 Doctors
19% Group Practice, 6-50 Doctors
13% Hospital-Based
7% Medical School/University
6% Group Practice, 51+ Doctors
4% Group/Staff HMO
3% Community Health Center

Source: Center for Studying Health System Change. 2008 Health Tracking Study Physician Survey. Sept. 2009.

Medicare was set up in 1965 using the same model as Blue Cross/ Blue Shield with insurers paying hospitals (Part A) and doctors

(Part B) separately. In the beginning, doctors were paid what they charged, so there was no cost containment incentive, nor was quality figured in the payments. In 1982, when actuaries first warned that the Medicare Hospital Insurance Trust Fund would go bankrupt in five years, payment methods began to change. Hospital payments were fixed for a particular visit, no matter what services were provided, and thus began the pressure on hospitals to contain costs and their pressure on physicians to cut back. In 1992, the Sustainable Growth Rate (SGR) system was implemented to contain costs. The SGR formula would have created a cumulative 26.5% cut in physician fees, but Congress has delayed enactment every year.

Obamacare has two principals that are likely to stay at the forefront of healthcare policy: (1) the uninsured should have health coverage (this is generally the young) and (2) hospitals need to improve quality and efficiency.

> *"Health reform will therefore push physicians further in a direction where they are already heading—either out the door or away from the traditional, independently owned private practice model, which is becoming largely unsustainable, and toward a number of emerging practice models. These models will vary by region and market, and will include ACOs, medical homes, large medical groups, community health centers, and/or hospital employment."*

—The Physicians Foundation

OUR VIEW: While we endorse the need for more cost-effective care for seniors, we believe that the holistic view that our private general practitioners have of your individual health is a thing of the past. We believe that we will see the same erosion in care that we have experienced by the consolidations of other large institutions like banks, where the institution has an agenda and bureaucracy that has little to do with caring for you as an individual. Do we really want our physicians to be rushed, worried, and poorly paid? Access will suffer as young people choose careers other than medicine and older physicians leave the field.

PART VI:
TAKE IT OR LEAVE IT—WHY SENIORS CAN'T JUST BUY PRIVATE CARE

If Medicare is unable to provide the necessary coverage for seniors, the question becomes, what prevents seniors from paying privately for their care? The answer is that Medicare's own rules and regulations make it difficult for doctors to provide care to seniors outside of the Medicare system. Once each year, physicians must choose one of three contractual options that affect how they will be paid for Medicare patients:

Figure 6–I: Doctors Must Choose Participating, Non-Participating, or Opting Out

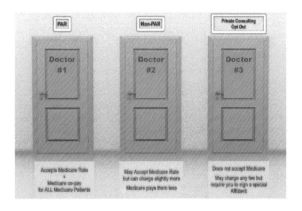

1. Participating physicians agree to accept Medicare's allowed charge plus a patient co-payment (80%/20%) as payment in full for all of their Medicare patients.

2. Non-participating physicians can choose to accept a 5% lower Medicare payment for some patients and not for others. They can also bill patients for more than the Medicare allowance for unassigned claims.

3. Private, contracting physicians can bill patients directly and "opt out" of Medicare. They cannot receive any Medicare payments on behalf of their patients.

It is not only Medicare that imposes these contractual obligations on physicians. Some hospitals and health plans require doctors to sign a participating (PAR) agreement. In addition, some states—including Ohio—have laws that prohibit physicians from billing anything more than Medicare allows. Medicare also incentivizes physicians to accept the PAR contract by paying them 5% more than non-PAR physicians, processing their claims more quickly, and giving them free publicity. However, physicians do *not* have to accept *all* Medicare patients who seek treatment from them. As more quality and performance requirements are imposed on physicians, will they choose to take more complex cases that might reduce their scores and therefore their payments?

Non-PAR physicians are prevented from billing more than 115% of their Medicare allowance (which is 5% less than PAR physicians) on fees not covered by Medicare. These non-covered fees are called "Balance Billing" as they refer to the amount the doctor is not reimbursed from Medicare. The American Academy of Family Physicians website indicates that "Non-PAR physicians would need to collect the full limiting charge amount, roughly 35% of the time they provided a given service, in order for the revenues from the service to equal those of PAR physicians for the same service."[234] In other words, the non-PAR physicians must look at their total book of business, including costs for collections, bad debts, and claims for cases in which they do not accept Medicare. Probably the worst part of the deal for non-PAR physicians is that the physician is not paid directly for cases where he or she chooses not to use Medicare reimbursement—Medicare pays the patient, thereby increasing the non-PAR physician's collection expense!

Figure 6-J: Opt Out Affidavit [235]

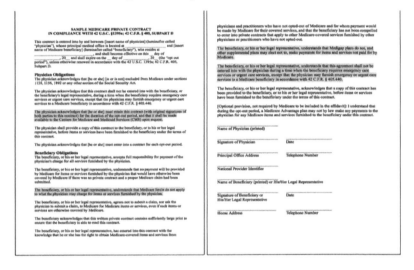

Understanding that some physicians may wish to opt out of the entire Medicare system, the private consulting physician (Opt Out) contract gives them the "freedom" to do so; however, Obamacare requires the physician to file a specific affidavit, signed by the patient, to Medicare Administrative Contractors (see Figure 6–J). If the patient of a private consulting physician requires emergency care, the Opt Out physician can only charge the Medicare limiting rate and may not bill or be paid for urgent care services.[236] Once

---

234 "Medicare Information from the AAFP," AAFP, http://www.aafp.org/practice-management/regulatory/medicare.html

235 Ibid

236 Ibid

physicians have opted out from Medicare, they are not permitted to accept Medicare for a two-year period. As you can see, signing this legalistic affidavit will likely make seniors worry that they will not receive the medical services they need. This contract must be in writing, must state that Medicare will not pay for the services, that Medicare supplemental insurance will not pay for the services, and that the patient agrees not to bill Medicare. The decision to opt out cannot be made on a patient-to-patient basis—it is applied to a physician's entire practice, and the physician may lose hospital privileges by opting out.[237]

None of these provisions prevent a physician from choosing to no longer accept Medicare patients.[238] These provisions are solely to deal with restricting how physicians may bill Medicare patients. That means that it may be easier for physicians to simply refuse Medicare patients entirely.

> **OUR VIEW**: Medicare has made it very difficult and costly for physicians to choose which patients can use Medicare as a payment method and, even more daunting, for physicians to opt out of the program altogether. We tend to agree with Dr. Field who argues, "Physicians are people who want to help people. They are not street crooks."[239] Doctors and patients should have a right to opt out of the system, whatever it is. If our healthcare system makes it too difficult for good people to practice medicine, the best will choose not to enter the profession or they will go elsewhere to practice. Medicine is a calling, which seems particularly evident when you consider that our medical school students generally leave their initial training with $250,000 in debt and then must spend an additional 3–7 years in residency before they become an attending physician.

237 Ibid.
238 Ibid.
239 Stanley Field, "Repairing the Healthcare System," http://stanleyfeldmdmace.typepad.com/repairing_the_healthcare_/2013/08/physicians-opting-out-of-medicare-and-obamacare.html

Another problem with the system is that doctors will be held to highly regulated measures of quality—and all the paperwork to go with it—which will make it less appealing for them to accept seniors who may have more complex conditions than what many seniors present. Medical decision making should be made by the physicians who have the experience and knowledge to make them—not by non-physicians following checklists based on rules-based decision trees devised by bureaucrats to control costs. Our best and brightest will end up off the grid. How will we follow them if Medicare prevents us?

THE TAKEAWAY: UNDERSTANDING WHAT THE FORECAST MEANS FOR YOU

- Medicare is already experiencing funding issues, which are only expected to get worse following the cuts that Obamacare will impose.

- Obamacare implements strategies to reduce the overutilization of healthcare through government bodies such as the IPAB, which will directly affect how much care you may receive. These new agencies and committees will oversee and advise your hospital and doctors about cost-savings opportunities.

- The government oversight in healthcare and focus on cost savings creates an inherent conflict of interest for doctors post-Obamacare, which may result in a difference in how long and how well you live.

- Medicare reimbursement cuts imposed by Obamacare will affect seniors and lead to less access to affordable care for Medicare recipients.

- The difficult rules that physicians are required to follow with regard to treating Medicare patients will result in fewer options for seniors seeking care.

Chapter 7:

Alternative Options to Increase Access to Care

We are facing a crisis in access to care, with none more acute than access for seniors. Access will be even more critical to individual seniors than cost, as 30 million formerly uninsured and uninsurable individuals seek to make up lost time, requesting services they were unable to receive from primary care doctors before Obamacare opened the door for them to enter the already-overburdened healthcare system.

Figure 7-A: Projected Medicare Enrollment

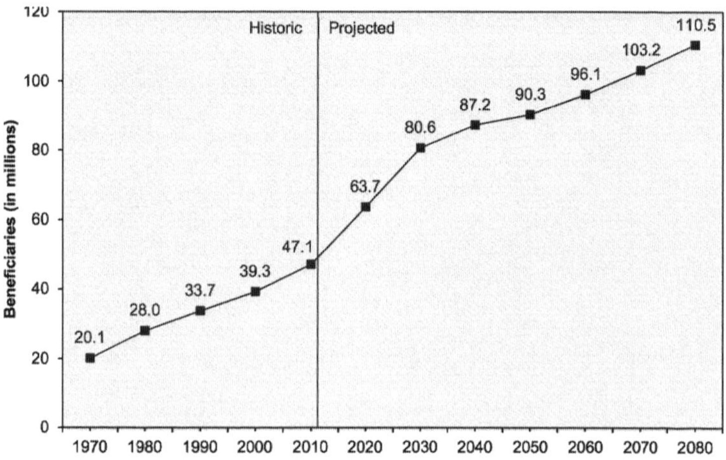

Note: Enrollment numbers are based on Part A enrollment only. Beneficiaries enrolled only in Part B are not included.

Source: CMS Office of the Actuary, 2012.

What can you expect? You will wait longer to meet with your primary care doctor as their schedules fill with the newly insured. You may have to travel further for your appointment to find a doctor who accepts payments from Medicare, as many doctors plan to stop taking Medicare patients in the face of new regulations and restrictions on how they practice and how they are paid.[240]

Once you have an appointment, you can expect 10–15 minutes with your doctor as Obamacare favors the "team approach" that substitutes nurses, physician assistants, and nurse practioners for doctor time. Once you are scheduled with your doctor, you must be prepared to cover the costs of potential procedures not covered by Medicare or insurance. As we learned in Chapter 5, the U.K. and Canada have long experienced these same problems with their healthcare systems. What have they done when they urgently need a doctor or their medical provider does not cover the necessary procedure? If they have planned ahead sufficiently, many have chosen to take charge of their own access to care by using alternatives to their overburdened national healthcare services. It follows from their experiences and choices that many of us will opt to seek alternatives if our own national healthcare is not up to the task of caring for us. The ultimate question is what you would be willing to do if your loved one had to wait a month for a critical diagnostic procedure or six weeks for radiation therapy for cancer or was unable to get a hip operation that might improve his or her quality of life.

In this chapter, we will explore some of the alternatives such as telemedicine, concierge medicine, and traveling for care. Some of these options can supplement plans available to Medicare beneficiaries, which will be a key to surviving the potential shortfalls Obamacare may create.

---

240 "More Doctors Steer Clear of Medicare," Wall Street Journal, http://online.wsj.com/article/SB10001424127887323971204578626151017241898.html

> **OUR VIEW**: It's a matter of trust. Perhaps the most troubling thing to us in writing this book has been facing the realization that seniors may lose trust in their doctors as a result of this new law. It is common knowledge that doctors have been one of the most trusted groups in this country. We believe that one of the reasons was that the fee-for-service model of the past, with all its warts, aligned the patient's interests of receiving the best care with the doctor's interests of providing the best care and being paid for it. Certainly there were some abuses and over-utilizations, but overall we think that most Americans believe that they have received the best healthcare of any country in the world. However, in the new Obamacare model of care, with its incentives to hospitals and physicians to reduce costs, will our doctors' interests still be aligned with their patients' interests of receiving the best care? Will the patients even know that they didn't get the newest and best scan, the more frequent mammograms or prostate screening? Will the doctors' recommendations be tainted by the requirement to save money, and, more importantly, will the patient even know it? We think many seniors will be looking for an opportunity to privately pay for a second opinion, and they may have to travel for the opportunity to do so.

PART I:
TELEMEDICINE—CARE FROM YOUR BARCALOUNGER

Imagine a year from now: you are sitting at home and notice your legs are swelling around your ankles. Instead of calling your doctor and booking an appointment for a few days from now, you set up a videoconference with him this afternoon. During the videoconference, your doctor logs into your home monitor. He checks your heart rate, blood pressure and weight to see if you are retaining fluid. He asks questions to see if you have leg pain. He makes his diagnosis. He prescribes and orders your medicine. If you had symptoms that warrant it, he can admit you to a hospital immediately. It might just save your life. This is telemedicine.

Bringing Technology and Medicine Together to Treat You at Home

If telemedicine sounds like space-age technology, that is probably because astronauts were among the first to use it. They sent physiological measurements to their NASA doctors back at home base during their flights nearly 40 years ago.[241] It solved a couple of problems for NASA, problems not unlike those you will face in the coming years as a senior under Obamacare. First, the ability to monitor your biomedical indicators can help your doctors stay ahead of potential problems, much as the mission control center needed to access these same measures to ensure that astronauts were responding normally in extreme and remote environments. Second, you may need treatment right away or you may need the hospital ready when you arrive for emergency care, much as the Houston doctors at NASA needed to provide care to their astronauts who were thousands of miles away from the nearest hospital and to examine and care for them when they splashed down.

Telemedicine has been used most extensively for remote access to rural communities and third world countries that would

---

241 "Telemedicine From NASA's Beginnings," Aerospace Technology Innovation, http://ipp.nasa.gov/innovation/Innovation53/telembeg.htm

otherwise not have access to medical care. As advancements in telecommunications continue, coupled with the demand for primary care and physician consultations, it is a promising alternative to face-to-face doctor visits.

Telemedicine encompasses a wide variety of delivery methods from simple e-mail exchanges and video chats to more complicated home monitoring with telemedicine devices that monitor your heart rate and vitals. It allows doctors and specialists to test, monitor, diagnose, and treat patients, in many cases, without the need for a physical visit, potentially reducing delays and supplementing traditional healthcare delivery systems. Cisco, Alcatel-Lucentare, Polycom, AMD Telemedicine, Cardiocom, Honeywell HomMed, International Business, LifeWatch AG, Robert Bosch Healthcare, and SHL Telemedicine Ltd. are the ten top-tier companies in telemedicine.[242] For example, Alcatel-Lucentare is working on using a secure web portal where "patients will have access to both scheduled and emergency care from any location at any time through a variety of mobile devices using real-time video and audio communication among multiple participants in multiple locations. At the same time, the system will securely generate, retrieve and store patient data in a clinically relevant way."[243] On the other hand, Cisco has been using its Cisco Health Presence Solutions technology to help "frail and elderly patients consult with specialists miles away without the stressful and costly ambulance rides."[244]

---

242 Andrew McWilliams, "Top Ten Companies in Telemedicine Technologies," BCC Research report HLC014E (Jan 2013) http://www.reportlinker.com/p01089680-summary/Top-Ten-Companies-in-Telemedicine-Technologies.html
243 http://www.upmc.com/media/newsreleases/2011/pages/upmc-alcatel-lucent-to-develop-telemedicine-solution.aspx
244 "Bridging the Distance: Telemedicine Extends the Reach of Healthcare in Europe," Cisco, http://www.cisco.com/web/strategy/docs/healthcare/10CS2534_HealthPresence_Article_r3_012210.pdf

Basic Care Anywhere, Anytime at a Cost You Can Afford

You may decide that telemedicine is the best way to take care of many of your health concerns because it consumes less of your time and most often costs less. A Johns Hopkins study has hypothesized that "it appears we can use the same technology Grandma uses to chat with her grandson to provide her with valuable medical care in her home . . . If this proof of concept is affirmed, the findings open the door to a new era where anyone anywhere can receive the care she or he needs."[245] Telemedicine plans will allow seniors to avoid long drives and long waits in their doctor's office to simply get prescriptions refilled.

Telemedicine works perfectly for many of the minor illnesses and chronic conditions that draw most adults and children into a primary care doctor's office. "It's been proven to aid patients in the management of chronic diseases including diabetes and heart conditions, as well as improved the quality of life for seniors who may need frequent check-ins, but wish to retain their independent living."[246] For this reason, telemedicine has focused on geriatrics. It is likely to be the delivery method of choice for those who plan ahead and can avail themselves of these programs. Others will wait in line for most routine medical needs, as millions of baby boomers reach the age when they will need care and find it less available under the new healthcare reform.

---

245 "Telemedicine as beneficial as in-person visits for Parkinson's patients," Fierce Health IT, http://www.fiercehealthit.com/story/telemedicine-beneficial-person-visits-parkinsons-patients/2013-03-12#ixzz2hiimf5cA
246 "Telemedicine, remote monitoring set to hit $296.5M in 2019," EHR Intelligence, (April 2013) http://ehrintelligence.com/2013/04/16/telemedicine-remote-monitoring-set-to-hit-296-5m-in-2019/

Monitoring 24/7

Telehospitals or teleclinics are available today in large, established medical institutions like the Mayo Clinic, which offers rooms equipped with satellite equipment, telemedicine examination rooms, administrative conference rooms, and auditoriums wired for consultations in their branches in Jacksonville, Florida, and Scottsdale/Phoenix, Arizona.[247] The Mayo Clinic is reaching out to communities that need specialists or a second opinion but do not have access to these services or cannot afford to have them locally.

Telemedicine is also available through several companies that offer home consultations as an option. For example, Doctalker is a 24/7 service that offers services in their clinic, or via phone, video, or through visits to your home. "Anytime. Anywhere."—that is the mantra of telemedicine.

Telehome providers, such as The American Health Care Professionals (AHCP) and other companies focused on the elderly offer individual devices in your home so that a trained nurse can monitor your vitals each day. They also offer 24/7 nurses and clinicians to answer your questions about healthcare. [248]

> *Example*: Mrs. Smith is an elderly type II diabetic, unmanaged and prone to UTIs. She was living on her own when she fell and was hospitalized for a hip fracture. She was discharged and returned home, but she could benefit from monitoring that makes sure she is taking the correct medicine and ensures she receives help if she falls.[249]

---

247 "Telemedecine at Mayo," Mayo Clinic, http://www.mayoclinic.org/tradition-heritage/telemedicine.html
248 American Health Care Professionals, http://ahcpofva.com/
249 "Telehealth & Telemedicine in Senior Health Care," American Health Care Professionals seminar (January 2012) https://www.youtube.com/watch?v=hb-Rrk-hgZk

Considering that an estimated four out of five elderly individuals that fall at home will *not* or cannot call for help or press any help buttons, a monitoring system that is not dependent on her taking action seems critical. The service also records every time she takes her glucose and blood pressure readings so that her doctor can follow her status and look for abnormalities.[250]

Telepharmacy services are another type of telemedicine. In telepharmacy, "a licensed pharmacist at a central pharmacy site supervises a registered pharmacy technician at a remote telepharmacy site through the use of video conferencing technology."[251] According to the American Society of Health-System Pharmacists (ASHP), telepharmacy may be viewed as "the use of telecommunications technology" to oversee pharmacy operations and/or provide patient services" and "allow onsite pharmacy activities to be fulfilled even if the pharmacist is not physically located at the point of pharmacy operation or patient care."[252] This may be a way for you to get your medications without having to leave your home. An interesting program sponsored by ASHP provided telepharmacy services to Cambodian immigrants in Maryland and California. A local translator worked with the patients on a videoconference to facilitate communication with the pharmacists. In another program aimed at seniors in the community, one geriatric pharmacist, Amy Busker, was worried that her elderly patients would find the technology uncomfortable but was pleasantly surprised to find that they "basically think it's really neat." In some cases, a kiosk is set up to provide remote access to their service. The interesting thing is that both patients and pharmacists generally feel that the service allows them to develop a strong personal relationship.[252] It seems reasonable that

---

250 Ibid.
251 North Dakota State University, Jun 28, 2013, http://www.ndsu.edu/telepharmacy/
252 "Telepharmacy Services Bring New Patient Care Opportunities," ASHP, http://www.ashp.org/menu/News/PharmacyNews/NewsArticle.aspx?id=3875

you will receive more focused service if you are face-to-face with the pharmacist on a video rather than the next person in line at a crowded pharmacy.

Can these technology-based programs help you in the future? They certainly provide an alternative to allow you to remain independent longer. What does Medicare pay for today? According to CMS, a "limited number of Part B services" which are described rather cryptically in their Manual.[253]

PART II:
CONCIERGE MEDICINE: HEALTHCARE YOUR WAY

Concierge medicine gives you unlimited access to your primary doctor and any of the services provided in his or her office, without the rush and without a waiting line. This type of practice is also referred to as membership medicine, concierge healthcare, cash-only practice, direct care, direct pay, subscription medicine, direct primary care, and direct practice medicine. There are many models, but the main objective is to provide individualized care with a personal touch. Generally, concierge doctors see only 100 to 1,000 patients per year, compared to an average physician who sees 3,000 to 4,000 patients in a year. The idea is that you pay your primary care out-of-pocket and cover major medical through insurance. The average fee varies depending on the practice and the age of the member/patient. Most plans allow you to pay monthly or annually, depending on the practice.

---

253 "Medical Tourism: Treatments, Markets and Health System Implications: A scoping review," OECD, http://www.oecd.org/els/health-systems/48723982.pdf

A concierge provider, E. Barrow Medical Group, advertises their medical service as more "like it used to be." They advertise, "If you want to emphasize prevention, but still want your physician to be there when you need a doctor most, or if you have complex medical problems that cannot be addressed in an 11-minute visit, or simply don't have time to navigate through the current medical maze, then this is the type of practice to seek."[254] Concierge doctors provide typically 45- to 60-minute visits that allow their patients more in-depth, individualized treatment and prevention plans. Interestingly, Forbes describes these services, which were once targeted at the wealthy, as surprisingly affordable. The concierge medicine provider One Medical Group, based in New York and San Francisco, charges members only $200/year.

Forbes recently published an article about concierge medicine that projected that primary care physicians will soon be forced to see as many patients as possible.[255] They predict that patient visits will occur in hurried 10- to 15-minute appointments under Obamacare, which will provide reduced and declining reimbursement to providers as they try to accommodate the increased number of newly-insured patients entering the system.[256] Further, the *Wall Street Journal* says that Medicare recipients are the most vulnerable, leaving older patients with less care, limited face time with their doctors, and longer waits.[257] The article discusses one case:

Testimonial

Linda Popkin lives in New York, far from her 97-year-old mother in Florida. With their mother in a concierge

---

254 E. Barrow Medical Group, http://ebarrowmedical.md
255 "Is Concierge Medicine the Correct Choice for You?" Forbes, http://www.forbes.com/sites/paulhsieh/2013/03/27/is-concierge-medicine-the-correct-choice-for-you/
256 Ibid.
257 Ricardo Alonso-Zaldivar, Associated Press (Apr 2, 2011) http://www.mercurynews.com/rss/ci_17760766?source=rss

> practice, Popkin says she and her siblings have direct
> access to the doctor as needed.
>
> "If one of us calls the doctor, he calls us back," she said.
> "We are involved in all the decisions. We definitely have
> peace of mind that Mom is seeing a doctor she can speak
> to if we have any questions. I'm sure you've heard the
> horror stories about people calling the doctor and they
> can't get in for three weeks." [258]

MedPAC, a commission that advises Congress on Medicare, hired consultants to investigate concerns that concierge medicine might create a "caste system," creating problems in access to care for Medicare patients.[259] Obamacare envisions a team approach with patients meeting with nurses and physician assistants rather than individualized medicine with a patient-doctor relationship.[260] This may be a harbinger of changes to come that limit Medicare clients from taking advantage of these more personalized services.

Can Medicare beneficiaries participate in concierge care? A recent CMS Medicare bulletin was issued to physicians, suppliers, and providers admonishing them not to participate in concierge-type medicine for Medicare patients. Further, they threaten fines as it "abuses the trust of Medicare patients by making them pay again for services already paid for by Medicare."[261]

> OUR VIEW: Seniors should not count on concierge care.
> Concierge plans fly in the face of the "egalitarian nature"

258 Ibid.
259 "Spread of Conceirge Medicine Prompts Medicare Worries," The Huffington Post, http://www.huffingtonpost.com/2011/04/02/concierge-medicine-medicare-health-care_n_844042.html
260 Ibid.
261 "Alert About Charging Extra for Covered Services," CMS, http://www.cms.gov/Outreach-and-Education/Medicare-Learning-Network-MLN/MLNMattersArticles/downloads/SE0421.pdf

of universal healthcare plans. We have not run across any of these plans in our reviews of universal healthcare plans in Canada or England. We have already seen in Part VI of Chapter 6 how doctors can be punished by "coloring outside the lines" and taking private pay for Medicare patients. In addition, the characterization of these plans as a "caste system" and an "abuse of the trust of Medicare" by CMS make it rather unlikely that these beneficial plans will be available to seniors.

PART III:
TRAVELING FOR CARE—"WHERE YOU GONNA GO?"

If Medicare denies coverage for your new hip or pays only a fraction for your heart stent, what will you do? Traveling for care may be your only option—and many are finding it the best choice. Individuals are going abroad for care in record numbers because the cost is right and the care is as good or better than they would receive in the U.S.

Although people have been traveling for health concerns for centuries, modern travel for care was prompted by the increase in healthcare costs beginning in the 1980s. "Tooth tourism" grew rapidly as patients traveled to countries like Costa Rica for dental bridges and caps not covered by their insurance.[262] Countries like India, Thailand, and South Korea as well as European and Latin American countries saw the promise of business and invested heavily in a medical infrastructure that could support eye surgeries, cosmetic procedures, and heart procedures. "The global

---

262 "Medical Tourism," Time, http://www.time.com/time/health/article/0,8599,1861919,00.html

growth in the flow of patients and health professionals as well as medical technology, capital funding and regulatory regimes across national borders has given rise to new patterns of consumption and production of healthcare services over recent decades."[263]

In the last decade traveling for care has been a competitive field with huge investments, big marketing campaigns and strong government support. The Canadian, British, and American markets (10% of the market) are a thriving force of the demand, along with a growing Asian market. Destinations providing care are spread out by specialty, geography, cost, and quality.

When Medicare patients are denied medical treatment at any cost and are denied medical freedom and access to services like concierge medicine, it seems reasonable to assume that traveling for care will flourish.

The Cost Savings Are Real

Cost saving is a compelling reason for patients to travel out of the country for care. In fact, patients are saving enough money on procedures that they can pay for their airfare and still have less out-of-pocket expense than their reimbursement for insurance. A full range of services is available from routine check-ups to diagnostic tests to high-tech surgeries. Popular procedures that are priced to make it worth traveling include:

- Orthopedic surgery (hip replacement, resurfacing, knee replacement, joint surgery)

- Dentistry (cosmetic and reconstruction)

---

263 "Medical Tourism: Treatments, Markets and Health System Implications: A scoping review," OCED, http://www.oecd.org/els/health-systems/48723982.pdf

- Cardiology/cardiac surgery (bypass, valve replacement)

- Organ, cell, and tissue transplantation (organ transplantation, stem cell)

- Eye surgery

- Diagnostics and check-ups

As cost is a major motivator, Figure 7–B below compares costs by procedure by country.[264]

Figure 7–B: Surgery Costs by Country

Surgery	USA	Mexico	India	Singapore	Thailand	South Korea
Heart Bypass	$144,400	$20,000	$10,000	$20,000	$24,000	$24,000
Angioplasty	$57,000	$15,000	$11,000	$13,000	$7,000	$19,600
Heart Valve Replacement	$170,000	$18,000	$9,500	$13,000	$22,000	$36,000
Hip Replacement	$50,000	$13,125	$9,000	$11,000	$14,000	$16,450
Hip Resurfacing	$50,000	$12,800	$8,250	$12,000	$16,000	$20,900
Knee Replacement	$50,000	$10,650	$8,500	$13,000	$12,000	$17,800
Spinal Fusion	$100,000	$7,000	$5,500	$9,000	$11,000	$17,300
Dental Implant	$2,000-$10,000	$950	$1,100	$1,500	$3,000	$3,400

EXPERTISE AND HIGH-TECH EQUIPMENT

In addition to cost savings, these travelers are receiving care by some of the best physicians in the world and are treated with state-of-the-art equipment. Many international hospitals are associated with leading hospitals in the U.S.; for example, "Johns Hopkins has

---

264 Ibid.

a research center in Singapore and Cleveland Clinic has planted its flag in the Middle East with its venture in Abu Dhabi, among other places."[265] In addition, Cornell, Duke, Harvard, Memorial Sloan Kettering, University of Pittsburgh, Columbia, and others have affiliates throughout the world.[266]

Further, some hospitals are American-owned and managed. For example, Dallas-based International Hospital Corporation operates four hospitals in Mexico.[267] The qualifications of staff in leading international hospitals are well recognized. Some of their physicians are trained in top U.S. and European programs such as Cleveland Clinic, Massachusetts General (Harvard), Johns Hopkins, UCLA, Oxford University, and Cambridge University, among others.

So Many Options—How to Choose

Today's top destinations are (but not limited to): Costa Rica, Hungary, India, Malaysia, Mexico, Singapore, South Korea, Thailand, and Barbados. Most countries are known for their expertise in specific procedures, which are listed in Figure 7–C.

265 "Mayo Clinic going global? Announces plans to expand in India" Medcity News (Sep 2011) http://medcitynews.com/2011/09/mayo-clinic-going-global-announces-plans-to-expand-in-india/

266 "Medical Tourism, Consumers in Search of Value," Deloitte, http://www.deloitte.com/assets/Dcom-unitedStates/Local%20Assets/Documents/us_chs_MedicalTourismStudy(3).pdf

267 Thomas Black, "Mexico Builds Hospitals to Lure Medical Tourists From America," Bloomberg (2008) http://www.bloomberg.com/apps/news?pid=newsarchive&sid=audTNhIlsFSg

Figure 7–C: Treatment Specialties by Country

Country	Treatment Specialties
Costa Rica	Cosmetic Surgery, Dentistry, Ophthalmology, Orthopedics, Weight Loss
Hungary	Dentistry
India	Cardiology, Cosmetic Surgery, Dentistry, Fertility/Reproduction, General Surgery, Neurology, Ophthalmology, Orthopedics, Stem Cells, Transplant, Weight Loss
Malaysia	Cardiology, Cosmetic Surgery, Dentistry, Fertility/Reproduction Health, General Surgery, Ophthalmology, Orthopedics, Stem Cells, Transplant
Mexico	Cosmetic Surgery, Dentistry, Ophthalmology, Orthopedics, Weight Loss
Singapore	Cardiology, Gastroenterology, General Surgery, Hepatology, Neurology, Oncology, Ophthalmology, Orthopedics, Stem Cell Therapy
South Korea	Cardiology, Dentistry, Ophthalmology, Orthopedics
Thailand	Cardiology, Cosmetic Surgery, Dentistry, Gender Reassignment, Neurology, Oncology, Ophthalmology, Orthopedics, Weight Loss
Barbados	Fertility Reproduction Health, Addiction Recovery

How do you choose a destination that's right for you? You may prefer traveling to destinations where you feel comfortable with the language and culture and where the costs are within reach. Understand that most hospitals have staff who speak English, and many are Americans who are drawn to the close client interaction and state-of-the-art medical technology. Other factors you should consider include the hospital's access to high-quality medical technology, the overall experience rating of others who have been there, as well as ratings for the clinic's staff experience and training. Before choosing a country and a hospital, you will want to make sure that the hospitals you choose are accredited by the Joint Commission International (JCI), which is the most recognized and recommended by the Center for Disease Control and Prevention (CDC). According to the CDC, as of March 2012, JCI has accredited 368 international hospitals in 46 countries.[268] The mission of JCI is to continuously improve the safety and

---

268 C. Virginia Lee and Victor Balaban, "Medical Tourism," CDC (August 1, 2013) http://wwwnc.cdc.gov/travel/yellowbook/2014/chapter-2-the-pre-travel-consultation/medical-tourism

quality of care in the international healthcare community through the provision of education and advisory services and international accreditation and certification. Quality Healthcare Trent Accreditation is the second-most recognized. You should find the following in all accredited programs:

- Professionally conducted surveys and peer-reviews

- A process to identify and correct problems for continuous improvement

- A process to ensure that action is taken on recommendations

- Periodic, repeated assessments every two to four years

"Accreditation is generally accepted to apply to organizations rather than individuals, although it can apply as readily to a dental clinic as to a full hospital. Accreditation has come to be thought of as a stamp of approval verifying the authenticity and quality of the services provided."[269] Seeking out an accredited hospital or clinic is an important part of your research.

> *Example*: Paul H., from Texas went to Monterrey, Mexico, for a meniscus-tear knee surgery. Paul chose Patients Beyond Borders as his facilitator after "not a single anesthesiologist would consider using an epidural instead of general anesthesia [in the U.S.]." Not having any insurance coverage, cost was also a factor. He decided to go to Mexico where his surgery would be more affordable. In the end his surgery cost $6,100 including air fare and accommodations, compared to $30,000 in Texas.

269 "Medical Tourism: Treatments, Markets and Health System Implications: A scoping review," OECD, http://www.oecd.org/els/health-systems/48723982.pdf

Paul chose a JCI-accredited hospital in Monterrey for his surgery. He chose his surgeon based on his qualifications and those of his team. "Paul's anesthesiologist was a graduate of the University of Texas and did his residency at Southwest Medical." His surgeon graduated from Baylor University in the top 2% of his class, completed additional training at St. Joseph's in Houston and at UCLA's Orthopedic Hospital, and is now one of the top orthopedists in Mexico. Paul flew in on Sunday, had surgery Monday, and flew back Tuesday. He describes his experience as very personal, economical, and quick. "All I did was talk to the international patient department, book my surgery, and book my own airfare. Simple. Two very short flights and I was there."[270]

If you would like to watch a "60 minute" segment with some patient comments you may want to watch the following the 60 Minutes Medical Tourism Video, available at http://www.youtube.com/watch?v=uSNsnKLUCdg.

How Do I Get There?

To make the process of traveling for care as easy as booking a vacation, there are American facilitators that help with the process. Some specialize by procedure and some by country, while others have a more generalized approach. Facilitators' experience can help evaluate your options, introduce you to the hospitals and doctors, and coordinate your trip by booking transportation and arranging for hospitality during recovery. To compare the destinations and doctors, there are some important questions you should ask your facilitator to provide: (1) measurable medical outcomes, (2) patient

---

270   Planet   Hospital   testimonial,   http://www.planethospital.com/testimonials.jsp#. UgREDGRgaft

satisfaction surveys, (3) patient improvement and functional health measures, and (4) infection rates.

A good example of how a facilitator helps clients is the experience of Craig Wright. He suffers from symptomatic Tarlov cysts, a rare condition recognized by the National Organization of Rare Diseases. His insurance denied coverage for the treatment that he needed, saying it was not necessary. Worried that he would have to live for years on various strong pain medications and with the possibility of paralysis, he turned to Planet Hospital for help.

A facilitator at Planet Hospital spoke to Craig and then sent his films and information to dozens of surgeons all over the world who were qualified for the procedure. Soon after, Planet Hospital replied with two all-inclusive quotations from different surgeons in Germany and India. Next, Planet Hospital arranged for surgeons to call him for phone consultations. He spoke to Dr. B. Walia and checked the surgeon's excellent credentials. The hospital was also rated higher in sanitation and quality of service than most hospitals in the U.S. After five days in India he was discharged with a successful surgery. He spent four more days in a five star hotel before returning for one last check up. The total cost with his expenses including airfare for two, surgery, all hospital costs, medications, hotels, meals, and shopping was only $20,000, about 80% less than the U.S.[271]

AMERICAN MEDICAL TOURISM BY THE NUMBERS

"In April 19, 2009, Gallop conducted a poll of 5,050 Americans about their willingness to leave the U.S. and travel overseas for

---

271 Ibid.

medical care. They found that up to 29% of Americans would consider traveling abroad for medical procedures such as heart bypass surgery, hip or knee replacement, plastic surgery, cancer diagnosis and treatment, or alternative medical care, even though all are routinely done in the United States."[272] That number is expected to increase as waiting lines and costs increase domestically. American patients who have gone overseas for care report high levels of satisfaction with the quality of care they receive. Most patients that travel for care rate their hospital care as excellent. When asked to compare the personalized service to that of a U.S. hospital, 85% replied their experience was more personalized and 15% said it was less.[273]

Figures 7–D and 7–E illustrate how actual patients reported about their experience in a survey done by the Medical Tourism Association. They found that 63% of patients that travel abroad felt their overall medical experience was better than it would of have been in the U.S., 37% found it to be about the same, and 0% felt it was less.[274] In addition, 93% of patients would recommend that a friend, family member, or acquaintance travel abroad for medical treatment. Figure 7–F shows that 90% also replied they would travel internationally again for medical services. Of the patients that took the survey 42% already had insurance, compared with 58% who had no insurance to cover the procedure. One might conclude that those with insurance had premiums higher than traveling abroad for care.[275]

---

272 Renee-Marie Stephano and Jonathan Edelheit, Medical Tourism: An International Healthcare Guide For Insurers, Employers and Governments (Kindle, 2010).
273 Ibid.
274 Ibid.
275 Ibid.

Figures 7–D: Comparison Figure. 7–E: Recommend Figure, 7–F: Travel Again?

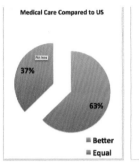
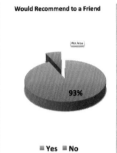
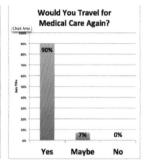

In summary, seniors face a myriad of challenges in accessing the healthcare that will allow them to remain independent in the future. This is particularly true as baby boomers reach the age where they need and demand healthcare. Baby boomers will not "go quietly into the night," rather, they will demand alternatives if Medicare or high deductible insurance are not there to cover their broken hips, chronic conditions, and other age-related conditions. The increase in the number of seniors and the cutbacks in reimbursements for Medicare doctors and hospitals surely mean a proliferation of some of the technologies and alternatives discussed in this chapter.

THE TAKEAWAY: YOU HAVE OPTIONS!

- There are both domestic and international alternative options for care for seniors who become fed up with Medicare.

- Domestic alternatives such as telemedicine plans can increase access to medical care by reducing long waits.

- International hospitals can provide a less-expensive and superior-quality alternative for seniors who seek increased access to care for everything from checkups to surgeries.

THE POST-OBAMACARE
RETIREMENT PLAN CHECKLIST

☑	Learn about the issues that affect you post-Obamacare.
☐	Consult with a professional to assess how your current retirement plan addresses the two predominant issues for seniors post-Obamacare: 1. How Will I Afford Care? 2. How Will I Access Care?
☐	Update your estate plan to save your money—don't pay unnecessary taxes under the new tax laws.
☐	Integrate Asset Protection Trusts into your planning to ensure that your personal and business assets are protected from liabilities and rising healthcare costs.
☐	Create protected side funds that can be used to pay for future care.
☐	Use longevity planning that incorporates pension-claiming strategies, whether for Social Security, public pensions, or both, so that you can optimize your income throughout retirement to provide a perpetual healthcare safety net and ensure that you do not outlive your assets.
☐	Learn from the lessons of countries, such as the Canada and the U.K., and the state of Massachusetts, all of which have similar healthcare systems, so that you know what to expect.
☐	In your healthcare planning take into account how Medicare will be affected by the cuts under Obamacare and in turn how it will affect the traditional model for seniors in accessing care.
☐	Incorporate planning that will allow you to utilize alternate options for accessing care, both domestic and international, that are much less expensive and more accessible than what you may be able to get following the significant Medicare cuts.

KEY REFERENCES

1. Public Law 111–148—Patient Protection and Affordable Care, aka PPACA, ACA, Obamacare

2. Nick Tate, *The Obamacare Survival Guide* (Humanix Books: 2013).

3. Betsy McCaughey, Ph.D., *Beating Obamacare: Your Handbook for Surviving the New Health Care Law* (Regnery Publishing, Inc.: 2013).

4. Rick Liuag, "The Obamacare Bootcamp & Handbook," http://obamcarebootcampconsultants.ssmedplans.com

5. 60 Minutes: Medical Tourism, http://www.youtube.com/watch?v=uSNsnKLUCdg

6. The Henry J. Kaiser Family Foundation, http://www.kff.org

7. Josef Woodman, *Patients Beyond Borders, Everybody's Guide to Affordable World-Class Medical Travel, Second Edition.* (Healthy Travel Media: 2008).

8. The Physician's Foundation, Health Reform and the Decline of Physician Private Practice: A White Paper Examining the Effects of the Patient Protection and Affordable Care Act on Physician Practices in the United States. Prepared by Merritt Hawkins (2010).

9. William Reichenstein and William Meyer, *Social Security Strategies: How to Optimize Retirement Benefits* (Perfect Paperback: 2011).